THE SPIRIT-FILLED FAMILY

Holy Wisdom to Build Happy Homes

Jack W. Hayford

with

Rebecca Hayford Bauer

THOMAS NELSON PUBLISHERS
Nashville • Atlanta • London • Vancouver

DEDICATION

This, the third series of *Spirit-Filled Life
Bible Study Guides,* is dedicated to the
memory of

Dr. Roy H. Hicks, Jr.
(1944–1994)

one of God's "men for all seasons,"
faithful in the Word, mighty in the Spirit,
leading multitudes into the love of God
and the worship of His Son, Jesus Christ.

Unto Christ's glory and in Roy's memory,
we will continue to sing:

Praise the Name of Jesus,
Praise the Name of Jesus,
He's my Rock, He's my Fortress,
He's my Deliverer, in Him will I trust.
Praise the Name of Jesus.

Words by Roy Hicks, Jr., © 1976 Latter Rain Music. Administered by The Sparrow Corp.
All Rights Reserved. Used by Permission.

The Spirit-Filled Family:
Holy Wisdom to Build Happy Homes
Copyright © 1994 by Jack W. Hayford

Published in Nashville, Tennessee, by Thomas Nelson, Inc.

Unless otherwise indicated, Scripture quotations are from the
New King James Version of the Bible, © 1979, 1980, 1982,
Thomas Nelson, Inc., Publishers

Printed in the United States of America
4 5 6 7 8 — 00 99 98 97 96 95

CONTENTS

The Spirit-Filled Family: Holy Wisdom to Build Happy Homes is one of a series of study guides that focus exciting, discovery-geared coverage of Bible book and power themes—all prompting toward dynamic, Holy Spirit-filled living.

About the Executive Editor

JACK W. HAYFORD, noted pastor, teacher, writer, and composer, is the Executive Editor of the complete series, working with the publisher in the conceiving and developing of each of the books.

Dr. Hayford is Senior Pastor of The Church On The Way, the First Foursquare Church of Van Nuys, California. He and his wife, Anna, have four married children, all of whom are active in either pastoral ministry or vital church life. As Executive Editor of the *Spirit-Filled Life Bible,* Pastor Hayford led a four-year project, which has resulted in the availability of one of today's most practical and popular study Bibles. He is author of more than twenty books, including *A Passion for Fullness, The Beauty of Spiritual Language, Rebuilding the Real You,* and *Prayer Is Invading the Impossible.* His musical compositions number over four hundred songs, including the widely sung "Majesty."

About the Writer

REBECCA HAYFORD BAUER is a housewife, mother, and writer, whose husband Scott is Executive Associate Pastor at The Church On The Way in Van Nuys, California. Besides serving as an editorial assistant to the Graphics Department at the church, a team she formerly led before motherly duties demanded more of her time, Becki is a writer in her own right. With her skills, she is often the key to the release of many books by her father, Pastor Jack Hayford.

She is a graduate of LIFE Bible College and has done post-graduate studies in writing at Pierce College in Los Angeles. Rebecca and Scott began their family just as he was completing study at Fuller Seminary, and they moved to Central California to take their first pastorate. They have three children: Brian, Kyle, and Lindsey.

Of this contributor, the Executive Editor has remarked: "It is heartwarming enough to see your daughter committed to Christ and the ministry, but all the more so because she is such a disciplined believer, devoted wife, diligent servant, and dedicated mother. She writes on family themes from a base of solid experience and genuine success as a wife and mom."

THE KEYS
THAT KEEP ON FREEING

> *And I will give you the keys of the kingdom of
> heaven, and whatever you bind on earth will be bound
> in heaven, and whatever you loose on earth will be loosed
> in heaven.* (Matt. 16:19)

While there is no conclusive list of exactly what keys Jesus
was referring to, it is clear that He did confer upon His
church—upon *all* who believe—the access to a realm of spiritual partnership with Him in the dominion of His kingdom.
The "keys" to this partnership are *concepts*—biblical themes
that promote spiritual vitality when applied with soundly based
faith under the lordship of Jesus Christ. The "partnership" is
the *essential* feature of this release of divine grace; (1) believers
reach to *receive* Christ's promise of "kingdom keys," (2) while
choosing to *believe* in the Holy Spirit's readiness to unleash
their power today.

Companions to the Bible book studies in the *Spirit-Filled
Life Study Guide* series, the Kingdom Dynamic studies present
a variety of different themes. This series is an outgrowth of the
Kingdom Dynamics themes included throughout the *Spirit-
Filled Life Bible*.

The central goal of this series of study guides is to help
you discover "power points" of the Holy Spirit-filled life.
Assisting you in your discoveries are a number of helpful features. Each study guide has twelve to fourteen lessons, each
arranged so you can plumb the depths or skim the surface,
depending upon your needs and interests. The study guides
contain major lesson features, each marked by a symbol and
heading for easy identification.

WORD WEALTH

The WORD WEALTH feature provides important definitions of key terms.

 BEHIND THE SCENES

BEHIND THE SCENES supplies information about cultural beliefs and practices, doctrinal disputes, business trades, and the like, that illuminate Bible passages and teachings.

 AT A GLANCE

The AT A GLANCE feature uses maps and charts to identify places and simplify themes or positions.

 KINGDOM EXTRA

Because this study guide focuses on a theme of the Bible, you will find a KINGDOM EXTRA feature that guides you into Bible dictionaries, Bible encyclopedias, and other resources that will enable you to glean more from the Bible's wealth on the topic if you want something extra.

 PROBING THE DEPTHS

Another feature, PROBING THE DEPTHS, will explain controversial issues raised by particular lessons and cite Bible passages and other sources to which you can turn to help you come to your own conclusions.

 **FAITH ALIVE**

Finally, lessons contain the FAITH ALIVE feature. Here the focus is, So what? Given what the Bible says, what does it mean for my life? How can it impact my day-to-day needs, hurts, relationships, concerns, and whatever else is important to me? FAITH ALIVE will help you see and apply the practical relevance of God's literary gift. As you'll see, these guides supply space for you to answer the study and life-application questions and exercises. You may, however, want to record all your answers, or just the overflow from your study or application, in a separate notebook or journal. The Bible study method used in this series follows four basic steps. **Observation** answers the question, What does the text say? **Interpretation** deals with, What does the text mean? —not to you or me, but what it meant to its original readers. **Correlation** asks, What light do other Scripture passages shed on this text? And **application,** the goal of Bible study, poses the question, How should my life change in response to the Holy Spirit's teaching of this text?

If you have used a Bible much before, you know that it comes in a variety of translations and paraphrases. Although you can use any of them with profit as you work through the *Spirit-Filled Life Kingdom Dynamics Study Guide* series, when Bible passages or words are cited, you will find they are from the *New King James Version* of the Bible. Using this translation with this series will make your study easier, but it's certainly not necessary.

A word of warning, though. By itself, Bible study will not transform your life. Through Bible study, you will grow in your understanding of the Lord, His kingdom and your place in it, and those things are essential. But you need more. You need to rely on the Holy Spirit to guide your study and your application of the Bible's truths. He, Jesus promised, was sent to teach us "all things" (John 14:26; cf. 1 Cor. 2:13). So as you use this series to guide you through Scripture, bathe your study time in prayer, asking the Spirit of God to illuminate the text, enlighten your mind, humble your will, and comfort your heart. He will never let you down. He promises you!

Part One:
The Foundation of the Family

Lesson 1 / What Is a Family?

My wedding was beautiful!

I had dreamed of this day since I was a little girl. I had dated my fiancé for several years, and I had planned all the wedding details for months. And everything was going perfectly . . . until the pastor began to speak. "Marriage is not based on love," he began.

I stood there appalled! *How could he do this to me! What an unromantic thing to say!* But as he continued, I realized that I was getting my first lesson in Marriage 101. "Marriage is not based on love; it's based on the will of God." As a bride, those words had little meaning to me, though I understood their intent.

Now as a wife of almost twenty years, I know exactly what Pastor Ron meant when he spoke those words: the foundation of marriage (and thus the family) has to be built on more than a passing emotion—it must be built on the Lord.

The foundation, intent, and purpose of the family is clearly laid out for us in the creation of the first family—Adam and Eve and, subsequently, their children. Yet, the way the family was created to function was totally different from what actually occurred outside of Eden. Read Genesis 1:26—2:25 and list the characteristics and functions of the family as God originally created it.

1:26

KINGDOM EXTRA

These verses introduce a phrase that is the cornerstone of the biblical understanding of man: *image of God.* The *image of God* is presented first and foremost in relation to a unique social or community concept of God. "Then God [singular] said, 'Let Us [plural] make man in Our [plural] image.'" Many scholars interpret this use of both the singular and the plural as an allusion to the Trinity: one God, yet a community of Persons.

The "community" that reflects God's image is a special community: the community of a man and a woman. When God chose to create man in His own image, He created a marriage, a family. The community of the family is a reflection of the community in the Godhead. Its identity, life, and power come from God.[1]

1:28

2:7

2:8

2:15

2:18, 22

Humankind was to play a major role in subduing and ruling over the earth. God meant for the first couple to live as a king and queen, in complete harmony and equality, sharing joint rulership over the paradise He had created for them. In Christ, God wants to restore that capacity to rule.

KINGDOM EXTRA

The original order of man's environment on Earth must be distinguished from what it became following the impact of man's fall, the curse, and the eventual deluge (Is. 45:18; Rom. 8:20; 2 Pet. 3:4–7). The agricultural, zoological, geological, and meteorological disharmony to which creation became subject must not be attributed to God. The perfect will of God, as founding King of creation, is not manifest in the presence of death, disease, discord, and disaster any more than it is manifest in human sin.

Our present world does not reflect the kingdom order He originally intended for man's enjoyment on earth, nor does it reflect God's kingdom as it shall ultimately be experienced on this planet. Understanding this, we should be cautious not to attribute to "God's will" or to "acts of God" those characteristics of our world that resulted from the ruin of God's original order by reason of man's fall.[2]

Now, compare these contrasting passages and list how these characteristics/functions changed after sin had entered the world, destroying humankind's capacity to rule.

1:27 and 3:20

1:29 and 3:19

2:2-3 and 3:17

2:25 and 3:21

2:8 and 3:23

2:23 and 3:12

Sin in the Garden of Eden ultimately brought about all of the maladies of the human family. The couple began to focus blame everywhere but on themselves (3:12, 13), thus destroying their unity, failing to accept responsibility, and placing themselves in the role of the victim. Fruitless labor, pain, and strife all entered the family unit as a result of the entrance of sin and disobedience.

KINGDOM EXTRA

The woman is not *directly* cursed, although it is obvious she comes under God's general curse. Rather, there will be a major marring of her appointed roles as wife and mother. Maternity will be with great suffering, a particularly disappointing consequence to Old Testament women who saw large families as a sign of blessing. "Your desire shall be for your husband" is difficult in the Hebrew. Most likely the expression carries the idea that, remembering their joint-rule in the Garden, she would desire to dominate her husband. "He shall rule over you" asserts the divine assignment of the husband's servant-leader role. There is no evidence that this was ever intended as a diminishing of the woman's person or giftedness, but rather as a redemptive role assigned the husband toward the wife as a means toward reinstating this original partnership. Note: the passage does not assert male dominance over females. It does assign husbandly responsibility for leadership in the marriage relationship.

Adam is also spared a *direct* cursing. His major mistake was in heeding the voice of his wife rather than the voice of God. As the one having the greatest responsibility, his sentence is the longest and most comprehensive. "In toil you shall eat of it" [v. 17] notes a marring of man's fundamental role as laborer/provider; work shall be with difficulties and futilities (thorns and thistles . . . in the sweat of your face). This lifelong struggle will then end in death.³

FAITH ALIVE

As grim as the picture appeared that day, God was already in the process of activating the plan of redemption. Read Genesis 3:15 and answer the following questions.

To whom was God talking?

How was God going to cause redemption to come about?

How was this prophecy answered in Jesus' coming?

 KINGDOM EXTRA

[Genesis 3:15] contains the first proclamation of the gospel. All of the richness, the mercy, the sorrow, and the glory of God's redeeming work with man is here in miniature. God promises to bring a Redeemer from the Seed of the woman; He will be completely human yet divinely begotten. "That serpent of old, called the Devil" would war with the Seed (see Rev. 12) and would smite Him. But even as the Serpent struck at His heel, His foot would descend, crushing the Serpent's head [see Rom. 16:20]. In Christ's life and death this scripture was fulfilled. Divinely begotten, yet fully human, by His death and resurrection He has defeated and made a public spectacle of the powers of hell (Col. 2:15). This first messianic promise is one of the most succinct statements of the gospel to be found anywhere.[4]

 FAITH ALIVE

Read the following passages of scripture and list how God intends to restore individuals, marriages, and families back to His original plan for them.

1 Pet. 3:7

Compare the following verses to Genesis 1:26.

2 Cor. 5:17

1 Pet. 2:9

Rev. 1:6

Compare the following verses to Genesis 1:28.

Matt. 7:16

John 20:22 (Compare to Gen. 2:7.)

Gal. 5:22, 23

Compare the following verses to Genesis 1:29, and 2:8, 15, 22.

Matt. 6:25–34

Phil. 4:19

Compare the following verses to Genesis 1:27.

Psalm 133:1

Eph. 4:3

Matt. 11:28, 29 (Compare to Gen. 2:2, 3 and 3:17.)

Understanding God's intent to redeem marriages and families back to His original plan is essential to our understanding of how to live within God-ordained relationships. His original intent was for God and humankind to live in open and loving fellowship. Their fellowship with the Creator would then extend into their fellowship with one another, creating homes firmly established on a joint pursuit of God. Then out of that would flow their ability to rule over creation. Once the tie between God and the first couple was severed, not only did they lose their power of rulership, but their home began to disintegrate. Without that shared purpose and conviction, none of us can ever firmly build our homes on the foundation of Jesus Christ. Relationship with Him must come first.

Look up the following verses and write out what scripture says our foundation for life is to be:

Prov. 10:25

1 Cor. 3:11

Eph. 2:20

2 Tim. 2:19

 WORD WEALTH

Understanding the meaning of the word "foundation" as used in the Scriptures can give us some key insights on how to build our homes on the foundation of God. The Greek word, *themelioō, Strong's #2311*—literally means "to lay a basis for." While the Hebrew word, *yacad, Strong's #3245,* means to set; to found; to sit down together, i.e., settle, consult:—appoint, take counsel, establish, found, instruct, lay, ordain. *Yacad* suggests not only a physical foundation, but an agreed-upon body of beliefs as implied by the idea of instruction and taking counsel together.[5]

FAITH ALIVE

In Luke, Jesus relates a parable that gives wise counsel on how we should establish our homes.

Read Luke 6:46–49; then, based on the passage, list three things we can do to establish our homes on the Rock, Jesus.

Contrast that with what happened to the house that wasn't built on the rock.

In verse 47, Jesus talks about those who hear His sayings and do them. How does this compare to the man who "dug deep" to build on the rock?

What are some of the adverse factors in our culture that "beat vehemently" on our marriages and families?

How does Matthew 16:18 compare with this text?

The fact that Jesus Christ is to be the foundation of our marriages and families shouldn't be surprising when you consider that the identity of the family itself is in God. In fact, throughout scripture, God is spoken of as our Father, our husband, our brother. In His completeness, He can fulfill all relational needs in our lives. Yet He asks us to live out these relationships as a picture to the world of His great love for all of humankind. Unfortunately, the picture we present is riddled through with imperfections because we are imperfect people. But we can learn lesson after lesson about how we are to relate to our families by studying how God relates to us.

KINGDOM EXTRA

Humanly speaking, we link the identity of a husband, wife, and children to their particular family name. This, however, is only a surface identification. Family identity has a deeper root.

"Family" is a word that is rooted in God: God is *Father*—the Father of our Lord Jesus Christ. In Himself, God is a "divine family." This truth also expresses itself in the way that God relates to people. The Bible reveals this aspect of God's nature in rich and varied use of family imagery: God is our Father, God is Husband to His people, God is like a nurturing mother, Christ is the Bridegroom of the church.

When a man and a woman come together in marriage, God extends to them this name that in essence belongs to Him—the name of family. Husband, wife, and children live up to the true meaning of this name as they reflect the nature and life of the divine family in their human family.[6]

Further, the relational core of the family—marriage—is modeled for us both in the relationship between Jesus and the Father, and in the relationship between Jesus and His Church.

KINGDOM EXTRA

The relationship between God as "Head" and Christ as Son is given as a model for the relationship between husband and wife. When the Bible reveals how the Father and the Son relate to each other, it also gives us insight into how husbands and wives should relate to each other.

The following principles for the husband-wife relationship are illustrated in the relationship of Jesus and the Father: 1) Husband and wife are to share a mutual love (John 5:20; 14:31). 2) Husband and wife have different *roles* and accomplish different *functions* in the marriage (John 10:17; 14:28; 17:4). 3) Though having different roles, husband and wife are equal; they live in unity (John 10:30; 14:11). 4) Husband and wife *esteem* one another (John 8:54). 5) Husbands express love for their wives through *care, shared life and ministry, attentiveness* (John 5:20, 22; 8:29; 11:42; 16:15; 17:2). 6) Wives express love for their husbands by being of one will and purpose with them; by exercising authority entrusted to them with humility and meekness, not striving or competing; in a word, by showing respect both in attitude and action (John 4:34; 5:19, 30; 8:28; 14:31; 15:10; Phil. 2:5, 6, 8; see also Gen. 3:16; 1 Tim. 2:8–15).[7]

FAITH ALIVE

Look up the passages from John listed in the Kingdom Extra above. How can the way Jesus and the Father interrelate be applied in our relationships with our spouses?

Finally, look up and write out Ephesians 3:14, 15 as an encouragement and reminder that our families have to be founded on God—our perfect picture of what a family is to be.

1. *Spirit-Filled Life Bible* (Nashville, TN: Thomas Nelson Publishers, 1991), 5-6, "Kingdom Dynamics: Gen.1:26–28, God Created Man (Male/Female) In His Own Image."

2. Ibid., 6, "Kingdom Dynamics: Gen. 1:31, Before the Fall."

3. Ibid., 9, notes on 3:16 and 3:17–19.

4. Ibid., 9, "Kingdom Dynamics: Gen. 3:15, The Gospel's First Proclamation."

5. James Strong, *Strong's Exhaustive Concordance of the Bible*, (New York: Abingdon Press, 1890), 50 (Hebrew and Chaldee Dictionary) and 36 (Greek Dictionary).

6. *Spirit-Filled Life Bible*, 1791, "Kingdom Dynamics: Eph. 3:14, 15, The Identity of Family Is in God."

7. Ibid., 1734, "Kingdom Dynamics: 1 Cor. 11:3, Jesus and the Father Model Relationship for Marriage."

Lesson 2 / Fatherhood, Brotherhood, and Your Place in the Family

Pick up any newspaper, and you'll see numerous stories of people killing, molesting, and abusing their fellow human beings. What is even more unbelievable are the accounts of young people killing another teen for a jacket or a backpack—something so worthless in comparison to a life. We read about millions of abortions. There is a definite trend toward euthanasia. And we watch the images of war on television without the batting of an eye. Through it all, we recognize a tendency in our culture: life has become cheap. There has been a basic erosion of the understanding of man's intrinsic worth.

 KINGDOM EXTRA

Man is distinct from the rest of creation. The Divine Triune Counsel determined that man was to have God's image and likeness. Man is a spiritual being who is not only body, but also soul and spirit. He is a moral being whose intelligence, perception, and self-determination far exceed that of any other earthly being.

These properties or traits possessed by mankind and his prominence in the order of creation imply the intrinsic worth, not only of the family of mankind, but also of each human individual.

Capacity and ability constitute accountability and responsibility. We should never be pleased to dwell on a level of existence lower than that on which God has made it possible for us to dwell. We should strive to be the best we can be and to reach the highest levels we can reach. To do less is to be unfaithful stewards of the life entrusted to us. (See Ps. 8:4, 5; 139:13, 14.)[1]

Like all other dysfunctions of the family, murder and a worthless view of life flowed out of the brokenness and sin that were perpetrated in the Garden of Eden.

Read the account of the first murder in Genesis 4:1–15 and answer the following questions.

What brought about the initial rift in the relationship of Cain and Abel?

How do you suppose Cain and Abel were to recognize that the Lord required sacrifice in worship? (see 3:20)

 KINGDOM EXTRA

The covenant love of God required that innocent animals be sacrificed to provide garments of skin as a covering for Adam and Eve. This early foreshadowing of substitutionary atonement points toward the necessity of judgment upon the innocent to provide a covering for the guilty. Adam and Eve made a vain attempt to cover themselves with their own efforts by sewing together fig leaves. However, God's order provided covering by means of a sacrifice. Under the New Covenant, we are required to be clothed with Christ rather than with our good works (Gal. 3:27).[2]

What do you think about the fact that God responded differently to the two offerings presented? What lesson are we to learn about how we present our worship to the Lord?

KINGDOM EXTRA

The issue of blood sacrifice as being essential for right standing with God is conveyed through the offerings of Cain and Abel. Pursuant upon the founding lesson God gave in dealing with Adam and Eve's sin (3:21), Cain's vegetable offering, the fruit of his own efforts, was an offering of self-righteous refusal to live under God's revealed covenant. As Adam's attempt to use fig leaves for a covering was rejected, so was Cain's offering; but Abel's offering of a blood sacrifice was pleasing to God. God's sacrifice of animals in the Garden had established the blood sacrifice as necessary for approaching Him. Right standing before a covenant-making God was shown to be a matter of life and death, not merely a matter of one's good efforts.[3]

What warning did God give to Cain in v. 7? What do you think it means?

How did Cain respond? How should He have responded?

Although God rejected Cain's offering, do you think God's warning to Cain reflects God's interest and love for Cain? Explain your answer.

Was Cain interested in reconciliation either with God or with Abel?

Define what you perceive to be Cain's ultimate problem and then write down how he chose to solve it.

How was this a bad solution? Did Cain actually deal with the issue between him and God?

KINGDOM EXTRA

The theme of brotherhood emerges early in Scripture; and from the very beginning, it is clear that God places a high priority on how brothers treat each other. In this passage the question of responsibility for each other first emerges. Cain asks, "Am I my brother's keeper?" The word used for "keeper (Hebrew *shamar*) means "to guard, to protect, to attend, or to regard." Are we responsible? "Absolutely," is God's answer. Not only are we our brother's keeper, we are held accountable for our treatment of and our ways of relating to our brothers (blood and spiritual).

For Cain's sins against his brother, God curses him throughout the Earth, takes away his ability to farm, and sentences him to a life as a fugitive and a vagabond (v. 12). This clearly indicates that unbrotherliness destines one to fruitlessness and frustration of purpose.[4]

As we read through Scripture, we find that God's ways are always inclusive. He always reaches to draw people in, to touch them with His love—and He calls us to do the same. The problem comes when our ingrained sin nature presses us to be exclusive. "Exclusive" may be loosely defined as "elite, fashionable, select." But in a different usage, it can also be "restrictive, prohibitive, and limiting." In our efforts to be part of an exclusive group, what we are actually doing is restricting and limiting God's potential in our lives. He calls us to reach out, to love, to make our world bigger!

Read the following verses and tell how they show God's inclusiveness or God's desire for us to be inclusive.

Gen. 12:3b

Lev. 19:18, 34

Matt. 5:44

Mark 16:15

Luke 10:25–37

John 15:12

Rom. 5:8

Eph. 5:2

James 2:1–9

1 Pet. 1:22

1 John 4:7

 KINGDOM EXTRA

Second Peter 1:4 describes God's "great and precious promises" intended to enable us 1) to be "partakers" in His divine nature and 2) to allow us to "escape the corruption that is in the world." These graces are necessary to lift us above the decay of human nature and unto "brotherly kindness" and "love" (v. 7). Brotherly kindness dissolves personal infighting and ungracious ignoring of one another. It allows refocusing on our real enemy—Satan. Further, to master love is to receive and release *agape* love: that Christlike, unconditional gift that is full of affection, bursting with benevolence, and that provides a love feast to all to whom we minister in the name of Jesus. This text is a promise for those yielded enough to let these gifts flow: we can actually participate in the divine nature of God, which is elevated above the corrupt, divisive spirit of the world.[5]

Once we've recognized that God has called us to love and be responsible for one another, the next step is to realize that all of life is sacred—every individual at every stage of life. Life is sacred because it has been breathed into us by the Creator Himself. Thus, our value comes from our Creator. But should we choose to deny that Creator, denying the rest of humankind's value will naturally follow.

KINGDOM EXTRA

In Acts 17:26 the unity of the human race is clearly stated, for through Adam and Eve (Gen. 3:20), and then the sons of Noah (Gen. 9:19), all races and nationalities of men came forth. We all proceed from one blood, both figuratively and literally, for the same blood types are found in all races. Humankind is a universal family. "Have we not all one Father? Has not one God created us?" (Mal. 2:10). We live in a single world community. No race or nation has the right to look down on or disassociate itself from another. The apostle Peter said, "God has shown me that I should not call any man common or unclean . . . In truth I perceive that God shows no partiality. But in every nation, whoever fears Him and works righteousness is accepted by Him (Acts 10:28, 34, 35). There are only two divisions of humankind: the saved and the unsaved. Other differences are merely skin deep or culturally flavored, but all people are relatives.[6]

FAITH ALIVE

Look up Galatians 3:28 and write it out below:

How does God view us in relation to those around us?

How do you feel about the concept of total equality between every human?

Is this a difficult idea for you to incorporate into your life? Why or why not?

Are there areas of prejudice, intolerance, or partiality in your life toward one group of people? What are those areas?

Present these areas to the Lord and ask Him to help you have the mind of Christ that sees the value of each person and the heart of Christ who loves the world and desires to see every individual come to know Him.

If we truly believe that all of humankind is one family, then it will have to affect how we view different ethnic groups, minority/majority groups, age groups, and gender groups. We will no longer be able to tolerate prejudice among the races—whether you are a minority or a majority. Racism goes both ways. Our concern for all age groups, including those still in the womb and the aged who can no longer care for themselves, will flourish as we realize the sanctity of life and what every stage of life has to offer. And our understanding of the differences and similarities between men and women will be seen to complement each other, not compete against each other. In fact, the Bible, rather than being just a book about men of God, gives some stunning examples of godly women who functioned with great leadership and ministry skills.

Look up these verses to see other women leaders. Some of these women led nations, some of them simply led their families, but all of them had a mind of their own and moved with confidence in their knowledge of the Lord. List their names and what they accomplished.

Num. 27:1–11

Ruth 1:16, 17; 2:2; 3:9; 4:13–15

Esth. 4:10—5:2; 8:4, 5

Prov. 31:10–31

Luke 1:38; John 2:3–5

Luke 2:36–38

Acts 16:14, 15

Rom. 16:1, 2

To finish our discussion of the value of every person, let us look for a moment at the lives of the unborn and the value that Scripture places upon them. Look up the following verses and write down what they say about prenatal life.

Ps. 139:13–16

Jer. 1:5

Luke 1:39–44

Scripture also invites us to expect the generation to come with anticipation, storing up the things of God to teach and share with them.

Ps. 48:13, 14

Ps. 78:4–6

Psalm 145:4

KINGDOM EXTRA

Abortion is definitely wrong. It is the taking of a human life, for the Bible shows that life begins at conception. God fashions us while we are in our mother's womb (Ps. 139:13). The prophet Jeremiah and the apostle Paul were called by

God before they were born (Jer. 1:5; Gal. 1:15). John the Baptist leaped in his mother's womb when the voice of Mary, the mother of the Lord, was heard (Luke 1:44). Obviously children in the womb have spiritual identity. From the moment of conception there is a progression of development that continues through adulthood. God condemned the Israelites who were offering their children as sacrifices to the heathen god Molech. Such children were burned up in the fires of sacrifice (Lev. 20:2), offered to a god of sensuality and convenience. The same is occurring today, and by acting in this way we are saying that human beings are not worth anything. This is a terrible blot on our society.

The Bible is not more specific on the matter of abortion because such a practice would have been unthinkable to the people of God. For instance, when Israel was in Egypt, a cruel pharaoh forced the Israelites to kill their newborn babies. In the Bible this was looked upon as the height of cruel oppression (Ex. 1:15–22). The idea of killing their own children would have been *anathema* to the Hebrews. All through the Old Testament, women yearned for children. Children were considered a gift from God. Women prayed not to be barren. How could a righteous woman turn against her own children to destroy them? Abortion is not only unthinkable, it is also the height of pagan barbarity.[7]

 FAITH ALIVE

Look up the following verses on being created in God's image. What can we further learn about how we are to think concerning all of humankind who have been made in God's image?

Gen. 1:27

Gen. 2:7

Gen. 9:5, 6

Acts 2:4

What parallel is there between Acts 2:4 and Gen. 2:7?

1 Cor. 11:7

Eph. 1:3–5

Hebrews 2:6, 7

James 3:8, 9

KINGDOM EXTRA

Life was breathed into man by God. Man was made in the "image" of God, and after God's "likeness" (Gen 1:26; 9:6). Man was God's unique, spiritual, immortal, intelligent creation. Thus, God commands, "You shall not murder" (Ex. 20:13). To take human life is to assault the image of God in man. Human life should be respected and reverenced. Life, even prenatal life, is always a miracle; and no one should feel he has the right to shed the blood of an innocent human being. The word "require" (Gen. 9:5) indicates that God was doing more than simply stating a rule. He was saying that He will actually "pursue" (Hebrew *darash*) or "seek" a man's life in payment for the innocent life he has taken. Let no disrespect for human life invade any mind. Let us proclaim the value and the sacredness of life.[8]

1. *Spirit-Filled Life Bible* (Nashville, TN: Thomas Nelson Publishers, 1991), 6, "Kingdom Dynamics: Gen. 1:26–28, Man's Intrinsic Value."
2. Ibid., 10, "Kingdom Dynamics: Gen. 3:21, The Blood, the Covering."
3. Ibid., 11, "Kingdom Dynamics: Gen. 4:1–10, The Blood, Essential for Right Standing Before God."
4. Ibid., 11, "Kingdom Dynamics: Gen. 4:9, Responsibility for One Another."
5. Ibid., 1919, "Kingdom Dynamics: 2 Pet. 1:7, 8, Brotherly Love Flows from the Divine Nature."
6. Ibid., 1661, "Kingdom Dynamics: Acts 17:26, The Unity of the Human Race."
7. Ibid., 2003, "Spiritual Answers to Hard Questions" #17.
8. Ibid., 18, "Kingdom Dynamics: Gen. 9:5, 6, The Sacredness of Life."

Lesson 3/The Covenant of Marriage—Part 1

Jesus loves weddings! Whenever He's invited He happily attends. In fact, the Gospel of John records that Jesus' first miracle took place at a wedding (John 2:1–12). That day Jesus turned water into wine. What might have been a wedding feast disaster without an adequate provision for the guests, turned out to be the most famous reception in history. It is more than merely a beautiful and poetic act for Jesus to turn water into wine at a wedding celebration.

There are a number of simple, yet profound, truths that accompany this first of Jesus' miracles. The very fact that Jesus asks for water is noteworthy. His miraculous work is not based on some strange combination of exotic ingredients for His miracle workings. What He asks for is the single most common substance found on earth. There He begins the miracle, asking to be provided with that which is abundant and freely available. "Fill the water pots with water," Jesus instructs. It does not get any simpler than that. The rest is up to Him. He is perfectly willing to bless this wedding. And He is just as willing to bless any wedding where He is invited.

God's love for weddings and marriages has an obvious sense to it. Marriage is the first relationship God provided for in Adam's world. It's the beginning point for blessing in the human social order, and without it, families, churches, and society itself could not exist. The covenant of marriage is the single most important human bond that holds all of God's work on the planet together. It is no small wonder that the Lord is passionate about the sanctity of marriage and the stability of the home. This covenant of marriage is based on the covenant God has made with us. It is in the power of His

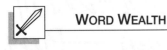

promise to her mankind that our personal covenant of marriage can be kept against the forces that would destroy homes and ruin lives.

WORD WEALTH

A covenant is a compact, pledge, treaty, or agreement. This is one of the most theologically important words in all of scripture, appearing more than 250 times in the Old Testament. A *berit* (covenant) may be made between individuals, between a king and his people, or by God with His people. . . . In Genesis 17:7, we see the greatest statement of the Abrahamic covenant. This is the foundation of Israel's eternal relationship with God. All other Bible promises are based on this covenant God made with Abraham.[1]

FAITH ALIVE

Who establishes this covenant in Genesis 17:7?

The Lord declares that this covenant shall be with Abraham and with his _____ (v. 17).

What is God's part of the covenant in this verse? What does God promise to do?

When does this covenant cease?

What is Abraham's responsibility in keeping this covenant, according to Genesis 17:10?

KINGDOM EXTRA

The act of circumcision was required as a sign of the covenant previously established with Abraham. This was not a new covenant but an external sign that Abraham and his descendants were to execute to show that they were God's people. The fact that this was performed upon the male reproductive organ had at least a twofold significance: 1) the cutting away of the foreskin symbolizes the cutting way of fleshly dependence, and 2) their hope for the future posterity and prosperity was not to rest on their own ability. Circumcision was a statement that confidence was placed in the promise of God rather than in their own flesh.[2]

The permanence of God's everlasting covenant with Abraham and his descendants is illustrated in Jeremiah 33:20–26. God is revealed as the Covenant-Maker. Here in this passage, God's activities in creation are described in terms of the permanence of His covenant. If the sun and moon do not perform their appointed daily course, and the seasons no longer occur, then the covenant with man will not endure. This passage continues by saying that if day and night do continue, *and* "if I have not appointed the ordinances of heaven and earth, then I will cast away the descendants of Jacob and David my servant."

Please notice that this promise of a secure covenant is given in the context of Israel's captivity into Babylonian bondage. Though the world is crashing in upon Israel because of their sin, God is still the covenant-keeping God.

 FAITH ALIVE

Read Jeremiah 33:20–26.

What is God's promise to the captive in Jeremiah 33:26?

How can God's keeping of the covenant with Israel be maintained in the middle of the national tragedy of Babylonian captivity?

Does the keeping of the covenant by God guarantee life in Israel without problems?

Are there times in your own life when the promise of God was difficult to hold onto in the midst of trying circumstances?

Are you in the middle of trying circumstances now which lead you to doubt God's promise of His goodness to you?

Read Jeremiah 31:31–34.

Jeremiah states the covenant was broken (see v. 32). Who broke it?

What do you think this new covenant refers to and how does it relate to Hebrews 8:8–12?

There is a powerful picture of the covenant-keeping God in Jeremiah 31:32. What is it?

If God is described as "husband" in v. 32, who is the wife? Does the husband remain faithful in light of the covenant-breaking of his wife in this passage?

Why does God use this powerful picture of marriage for His relationship with Israel?

What does the faithfulness of God in the covenant of marriage to Israel model for faithfulness in marriage in the church today?

     WORD WEALTH

In the New Testament the Greek word *diatheke* is used for the concept of covenant. A will, testament, pact, contract, and agreed upon plan to which both parties subscribe defines it. While the word may signify an agreement between two parties, with each accepting mutual responsibility, most often it is a declaration of one person's will. In the Bible, God initiated the whole action, set the conditions, and defined as a decree a declaration of purposes. God covenanted with Noah, Abraham, Moses, and Israel. In the New Testament Jesus ratified by His death on the cross a new covenant, termed in Hebrews 7:22 "a better covenant."[3]

This new covenant offers the promise of forgiveness of sin and eternal life to all who receive Jesus Christ as their Savior. We read earlier in Jeremiah 31:32 that the Lord's relationship with Israel was like that of a husband to his wife. Some of that same imagery is used in the New Testament.

Read Ephesians 5:22–33 and answer the questions below.

The parallel in verse 23 is between the husband as "head of the wife" and Christ who is head of the _____.

What is the Apostle Paul addressing in this passage of Scripture? (See v. 32.)

From this passage of scripture there are specific ways in which husbands are to relate to their wives as Christ relates to the church. What are they?

v. 23

v. 25

v. 26

v. 27

v. 28

v. 29

v. 31

THE COVENANT BETWEEN HUSBAND AND WIFE

The basic concept of Christ as a husband is one of self-sacrificing love and absolute devotion to His bride. This covenant relationship between Jesus and the church is unbreakable because the Lord is the One who personally maintains the union. This is possible because Jesus Christ is God Himself—divine, without sin, and unbroken by human weakness. But how are we to maintain our covenant of marriage between two people when there is so much human failure and limitation to overcome in each of us?

Read Genesis 2:18–25. The account of the first couple is profound in insight for all married couples. Let's examine some of the principles of what marriage at a human level is to be about. What was Adam's state in Gen. 2:17?

Why did God give Adam a partner in 2:18?

This passage of scripture points to significant areas of married life which hold keys to the success of the union. In verse 24 there are three specific considerations stated as being important in this union of man and woman. What are they?

1.

2.

3.

The challenge of becoming your own family—"a man shall leave his father and mother"—is a great problem in our society today. What are the consequences for marriage relationships that struggle with accepting the responsibility of being their own family unit?

What advice would you give a young couple that is financially dependent on one set of parents?

What is the impact on a marriage relationship when one spouse draws emotional support from parents rather than from his or her spouse?

The unity God has planned for marriage is illustrated in Genesis 3:9. What are the names of the man and woman in this verse?

When does the woman receive the name Eve?

Who names her Eve in Genesis 3:21?

In the social convention of marriage in our culture the woman almost always receives the surname of her husband in marriage. Do you think there is any spiritual significance to this practice?

Why would a woman prefer to retain her maiden name after marriage?

Is this appropriate? What are her reasons for such a decision?

Could the rejection of a husband's last name be related to a wife's desire to maintain independence from a husband?

Is this a valid reason for maintaining a maiden name for a couple?

In Genesis 1:26 God speaks and declares, "Let Us make man in Our image." So the perfection of unity as described in the Godhead is to be reflected in the unity God brings about in a man and woman who are united in marriage. Does unity in marriage demand that individual tastes, preferences, skills, and gifts be denied for the sake of oneness?

When personal preferences, ideas, or desires interfere with the marriage, what should a couple do?

The concept of unity in marriage is a beautiful truth. How does it become a reality in a marriage?

Are there things that couples can do to foster unity in their home? Name some of these things that create unity.

Name some of the things that break unity between husband and wife in the home?

Can you name couples in the Bible who demonstrate unity in their marriage relationship?

Read Malachi 2:15. The context of this verse is the tragic reality of divorce and the breaking of unity in marriage. The prophet declares God's Word concerning divorce. In this verse, who does the Bible declare to be the one who unites married couples, making them one?

If unity in marriage is more than simply a human attempt at getting along as described in Malachi 2:15, do you think God has any interest in maintaining the union of husband and wife? Why?

Read Matthew 19:4–6. Verse 5 refers directly to Genesis 2:24. However, Jesus adds verse 6 to the Old Testament passage. He expands upon the concept of the unity of the couple to be a God-ordained and executed unity. Literally, the unity God has planned for couples is actually accomplished through His work in them.

 **FAITH ALIVE**

Who does Jesus say does the joining? (See Matthew 19:6.)

How do you think this joining is accomplished in marriage?

We've all heard the phrase, "This is a marriage made in heaven." Why do you think God makes a personal investment in every marriage?

You who are married: Why does God take a personal interest in your marriage?

If you are a single person, do you think the selection of a marriage partner is merely a matter of falling in love?

What does the Lord mean in 2 Corinthians 6:14, "Do not be unequally yoked"? What does this imply in the selection of a mate?

It is not possible to live in unity with a marriage partner who does not share the same love for Jesus Christ that you have. You may be best friends and love each other deeply. However, the ultimate foundation of any marriage that is in Christ is Jesus Himself. The basis for all decision-making, child rearing, and life commitments for the Christian are all based in our life in Christ. Any person who does not share this fundamental faith in Christ can never fit into the most intimate part of your spiritual life. "Planning a marriage to an unbeliever will produce an unequal alliance that is to be avoided. To experience a happy union, the believer should align with one whose ideals and visions center in Jesus Christ."[4]

Jesus' words in Matthew 19:6 end with, "What God has joined together, let not man separate." What do you think Jesus means by this?

Do you think this also applies to people who want to separate from their spouse in times of stress or trial?

Do you think problems are avoided in times of separation between marriage partners experiencing difficulties?

Where can couples go for help if they find their marriage is under attack?

Where would you go if you needed help in your marriage?

Since Jesus says that it is the will of God for couples to stay married, whose will is it that couples separate and divorce?

Is it possible that in times of stress couples turn on each other because of the blinding work of the devil, instead of turning to the Lord for help?

What would you suggest to a couple who are experiencing deep marital stress?

How do prayer and your spiritual life affect the quality of your marriage?

SEX IN MARRIAGE

Let's take one more look at Genesis 2:24. What does the phrase "one flesh" mean in the passage? How important is the sexual relationship in marriage? In Genesis 1:28, God give man His first command—what is it?

The Bible states in 1 Corinthians 7:2–5 that married couples do not have authority over their own bodies. Further, it declares that a marriage partner is to give authority over their body to their mate. This is directly related to sexual union in marriage. Sex does not make a marriage, but many marriages have been broken over the subject of sex. (For more study on this subject see Lesson 10.)

MARRIAGE IS NOT NECESSARILY FOR EVERYONE

Our society has traditionally assumed that people would marry in the course of their lifetime. However, the Bible makes provision for some that will never marry. Often this is not the first choice of the individual, though for some it is. What does the Bible say about singleness?

Read Matthew 19:12. What are "eunuchs for the kingdom of heaven's sake?"

Jesus said that these people have a unique quality about their life from the womb. Do these people struggle with their singleness?

Read 1 Corinthians 7:7–9; 25–40. What does it say about singleness in verse 7?

Does everyone have this gift?

In verse 9 it gives one possible reason for marriage. What is it?

Do you think God is surprised by the strength of the sexual desire that is found in people?

Do you think that this sexual desire is part of God's plan to motivate some people to marriage?

Certainly, the desire for sexual activity is inadequate if it were the sole reason for marriage. However, in the search for deep spiritual meaning to their lives, some people overlook the very natural ways God has made them in their consideration of marriage.

When my husband counsels couples who are engaged to be married, he asks them if they "spark" together. You know, do they tingle when they are close to each other? On occasion he has had couples say no. These couples love each other, believe God wants them to be married, but they feel little, if any, sexual attraction toward each other. To these couples he always says the same thing: "Come back and see me when you start to spark together!" By that he doesn't mean he wants couples to engage in premarital sexual activity, but rather, he wants to know that they are well matched for each other spiritually, emotionally, intellectually, and physically. They need to feel passionately toward each other. It is *one* of the confirming signs of a good match for marriage.

Read 1 Corinthians 7:25–40 again. What does Paul suggest to the unmarried person in this passage?

In verse 28 does Paul claim it is wrong to marry?

Verse 34 suggests that unmarried people can serve the Lord more completely. What do you think about this for your life?

Do you think it is the Lord's plan for the majority of people to be single or married? Why?

If a person is to remain single all their life, does God see them as a whole person or as an unfulfilled person? (See verse 40.)

It is God's will for all people to be happy, fulfilled, and fruitful for His kingdom. If you believe that God has a marriage partner for you, then pray and live a holy life in anticipation of the answer to that prayer. In the meantime, live for Jesus; serve Him with all your heart; be a person who is thankful and joyous. And know that Psalm 37:3–5 is your answer from God.

Trust in the Lord, and do good; dwell in the land, and feed on His faithfulness. Delight yourself also in the Lord, and He shall give you the desires of your heart. Commit your way to the Lord, trust also in Him, and He shall bring it to pass.

1. *Spirit-Filled Life Bible* (Nashville, TN: Thomas Nelson Publishers, 1991), 29, "Word Wealth: Gen. 17:7, covenant."
2. Ibid., 29, "Kingdom Dynamics: Gen. 17:10, Circumcision's Significance."
3. Ibid., 1498, "Word Wealth: Mark 14:24, covenant."
4. Ibid., 1768, "Truth-in-Action through 2 Corinthians," #2.

Lesson 4/The Covenant of Marriage—Part 2

"But I thought it would solve my problems . . ." These heartbreaking words have been heard by pastors, counselors, friends, and family countless numbers of times. The divorce was supposed to answer the critical issue of a broken relationship between two partners who had "grown apart" and now face "irreconcilable differences." But the reality is that after the divorce the personal issues that broke the marriage still reside with each partner. Divorce may offer relief from a partner, but it is of no value in dealing with the personal needs an individual takes with him/her after the fact.

What does God say about divorce among the people of God? How do the realities of a world fouled by sin influence the church's stand on the issue of family and divorce? These complex matters have usually been dealt with by the church with either a legalistic rejection of the idea of divorce and divorced people, or with a casual indifference to the sacredness of marriage and the "cheap grace" which sanctions sin and its death-dealing results in families.

Read Malachi 2:10–17.

What was the "covenant of the fathers," verse 16?

God's concern for the stability of the family unit in Israel is marked by specific guidelines given for the selection of a spouse in Deuteronomy 7:1–4. What was God's concern in this passage?

How does 2 Corinthians 6:14 relate to the issue of selecting a mate according to the apostle Paul?

Read Ezra 9—10.

Compare the Ezra and Malachi passages. Note significant similarities and differences.

 KINGDOM EXTRA

The covenant relationship of marriage is highly esteemed by the Spirit of God. He instructs believers to seek a believing partner to ensure holiness in the marriage. He also requires just and faithful behavior within the marriage bonds. God hates the hard-hearted attitudes that destroy this sacred covenant and produce divorce.

Obey God; marry only in the Lord. Be loving and faithful to your marriage partner. Reject divorce as an answer to marital problems. Honor your covenant with God. Trust Him to recover the hope in a seemingly "hopeless" marriage. Be willing to relearn love, understanding, and forgiveness.[1]

Malachi 2 continues with strong words concerning divorce. Why does God say that He "hates divorce" in verse 16?

Who is the "witness" to the domestic problems of married couples, verse 14?

Who sanctifies the union between husband and wife, making them one, verse 15?

What does God "seek" in a marriage union, and what impact does divorce have on this desire (v. 15)?

The conventional wisdom of the psychological community declares that couples should not sacrifice their own individual happiness by staying together for the sake of the children. It is presumed that those who are unhappy with their marriage partners will be ineffective parents. Do you think this is true? Why or why not?

What two words does God use to describe the act of divorce in verse 16?

Malachi writes about the "covenant" of marriage in verse 14. Where does the concept of a marriage covenant begin in Scripture? (See Genesis 1:26–28; 2:18–24.)

Verse 15 implies that the Lord views Himself as an active participant in this covenant as well. Describe what you understand to be the Lord's place in a marriage and how divorce can violate our marriage covenant before Him.

Turn to Jeremiah 11:10, 11. Describe what the prophet says about God's view toward the breaking of covenant.

 KINGDOM EXTRA

When two people marry, God stands as a witness to the marriage, sealing it with the strongest possible word: *covenant.* "Covenant" speaks of faithfulness and enduring commitment. It stands like a divine sentinel over marriage, for blessing or for judgment.

Divorce is here described as *violence.* To initiate divorce does violence to God's intention for marriage and to the mate to whom one has been joined.

Yet, where husband and wife live according to their marriage vows, all the power of a covenant-keeping God stands behind them and their marriage. What a confidence, to know that God *backs up our marriage.* His power and authority stand against every enemy that would violently threaten it from without or within.[2]

Malachi declares that there are important consequences in our relationship with God because of divorce. What are they? (See Mal. 2:13, 17.)

 FAITH ALIVE

Since God is so vitally interested in the success of marriages and the blessing of His people, what might be alternatives to divorce for people who are severely stressed in their marriage relationship?

Do you think that all of your above suggestions line up with the standards the Lord lays down for us?

How would the fact that God backs up the marriage covenant affect any of those actions?

JESUS AND THE MATTER OF DIVORCE

The matter of divorce and the people of God was raging during the days of Jesus' ministry. The Old Testament teachings on divorce had been liberally applied by certain schools of rabbinic teaching. Shammai was a rabbi who taught that divorce could only be obtained if adultery were the cause. Hillel taught that divorce could be sought and received "for just any reason" even if it was as arbitrary as personal dislike of your wife.[3]

As a result of those attitudes toward the family, divorce had become increasingly fashionable in Israel during Jesus' time. Turn to Matthew 19:3–10. Who asked Jesus the question concerning divorce in verse 3?

What was the motive behind the question as recorded by Matthew in verse 3?

Do you think the questioner was sincerely seeking Jesus' opinion on divorce? Why or why not?

In verse 6, Jesus makes three profound statements concerning the institution of marriage. What are they?

Why is God so interested that married couples remain married?

From your understanding of verses 3–6, do you think Jesus approves of the concept of divorce?

Why does Jesus say, in verse 8, that Moses allowed for divorce?

      KINGDOM EXTRA

In Matthew 19, Jesus frankly addresses a pivotal issue: the cause of divorce is *hardness of heart*. Behind every broken marriage is a heart hardened against God, then hardened against one's mate. From the very beginning, God's intention for marriage was that it be for life. Realizing this, believers should exercise care in choosing a life mate (see 2 Cor. 6:14). Yet no marriage will be so free of differences and difficulties that it could not end up in divorce if husband and wife were deceived into following their natural inclinations.

The devil will exaggerate your mate's failures and inadequacies, sow suspicion and jealousy, indulge your self-pity, insist that you deserve something better, and hold out the hollow promise that things would be better with someone else. But hear Jesus' words, and remember: God can change hearts and remove all hardness if we will allow Him.[4]

Did Jesus contradict Moses in his teaching on divorce in Matthew 19:8, 9?

Read Leviticus 20:10. Why was the Old Testament punishment for adultery so severe?

How did Jesus respond to the woman who was taken in adultery in John 8:1–12?

Since the "woman was caught in adultery, in the very act," why was her partner not brought to Jesus as well?

What does Jesus mean by the phrase "but from the beginning it was not so" in Matthew 19:8?

FAITH ALIVE

In verse 10, the disciples exhibit an interesting response to Jesus' words about divorce. Could it be that the cynical and worldly attitudes toward marriage found in our world today were common in Jesus' day, too?

What affect do these cynical attitudes have on the institution of marriage in our culture today?

To what degree has the influence of the worldly perspective on marriage and family had an impact on believers in the church today?

HOSEA THE PROPHET ON DIVORCE

God illustrated His commitment to unfaithful Israel in the life and ministry of Hosea the prophet. Hosea, whose name means "Salvation" or "Deliverance," was chosen by God to live out His message to His people by marrying a woman who would be unfaithful to him.[5] The first three chapters of the book offer perspective on the graciousness of God in the midst of seemingly impossible circumstances.

Read Hosea 1–3. What is the sin of Gomer in Hosea 2:2?

What does God do to attempt to stop Israel's unfaithfulness in 2:6?

Is this a good strategy for any marriage partner in this situation? Why or why not?

What is Israel's motivation for returning to the Lord in 2:7?

What are the conditions for return to a relationship with the Lord in 2:9–13?

God is not interested in punishing Israel. The Lord desires to reestablish a relationship. How does 2:14–16 demonstrate this?

What are God's instructions to Hosea concerning his wife in 3:1?

What conditions for return does Hosea place on Gomer in 3:3?

PROBING THE DEPTHS

This chart shows the commitment of God to Israel as it is described in terms of a troubled marriage.

ISRAEL'S APOSTASY AND HOSEA'S MARRIAGE (3:1)[6]		
The stages of Israel's relationship with God are depicted in the prophecies of Jeremiah and Ezekiel, as well as in Hosea's relationship with Gomer.		
Stage	Israel's Prophets	Hosea's Marriage
Betrothal	Jeremiah 2:2	Hosea 1:2
Marriage	Ezekiel 16:8–14	Hosea 1:3
Adultery	Jeremiah 5:7; Ezekiel 16:15–34	Hosea 3:1
Estrangement	Jeremiah 3:8–10; Ezekiel 16:35–52	Hosea 3:3, 4
Restoration	Ezekiel 16:53–63	Hosea 3:5

THE APOSTLE PAUL ON DIVORCE

Read 1 Corinthians 7:10–16. Does the apostle Paul have different regulations concerning divorce for men as compared to those for women?

What does the Apostle Paul say about separation as an answer for marital problems in verse 10?

According to verse 11, what are the two options for a person who has deliberately left their spouse in separation?

What instructions do verses 11 and 12 give to husbands?

What instructions do verses 10 and 13 give to wives?

Does God require more from believers in a marriage relationship than He does from unbelievers?

List some of the reasons this is true?

In verse 14 the believing spouse has a radical impact on the state of the children. What is it?

What is required of a believing spouse if they should be abandoned by an unbelieving mate?

 FAITH ALIVE

Though God does not require an abandoned mate to wait for the return of a wayward, unbelieving spouse, many have prayed and waited for the return of a spouse only to see the miracle of 1 Corinthians 7:16 or 1 Peter 3:1 happen. The salvation of that partner and reconciliation in the marriage hinges on the unrelenting love and faithfulness which God places in the heart of the rejected spouse.

Such selflessness is only possible as a person draws on the day-to-day strength of the Holy Spirit who urges that mate forward in the struggle of faith. However, there are God-ordained limits to such pursuit of a wayward partner. Deuteronomy 24:4 clearly states that when a partner has remarried another person, God no longer supports the notion of reconciliation with the original spouse. The new married unit, regardless of its history, is to be maintained. Repentance and forgiveness are to be found within the context of the Lord's redemptive grace within the new relationship.

PROBING THE DEPTHS

The issue of divorce and "abandonment" as taught in 1 Corinthians 7:10–16 offers clear guidelines for the believer: do not divorce. However, the circumstances of some marriages may place a partner in serious, and at times even dangerous, positions where violence and abuse are a part of the home. The apostle Paul's words do not mean that a believer must accept brutality, physical abuse, neglect, or immoral treatment.[7] The Bible teaches that "there is safety in a multitude of counselors." Seek the counsel of your pastor and elders of your church to assist you if you find yourself in such a situation.

WHAT ABOUT REMARRIAGE?

Historically, many segments of the church have forbidden remarriage to divorced people. What does 1 Corinthians 7:15 say about the abandoned spouse?

What does Romans 7:2 say about the privilege of remarriage?

What does Paul say the Lord's preference is for the unmarried in 1 Corinthians 7:25–27?

Why does Paul use the phrase "are you loosed from a wife" in 1 Corinthians 7:27?

Who is the person "loosed" in 1 Corinthians 7:27?

Could the loosed person be related to verse 15?

What does Paul teach about marriage in 1 Corinthians 7:28?

How does this relate to 1 Corinthians 7:15, 27?

Jesus' words are very specific in Matthew 19:9—He forbids remarriage. To whom is Jesus referring in this verse?

Is Jesus, in this passage, forbidding the privilege of remarriage to the spouse who has been defrauded?

 FAITH ALIVE

Many have experienced the guilt and shame of infidelity and/or divorce. Even if you have been the party responsible for the breaking of your marriage covenant, there is forgiveness in Jesus Christ. There is only one unforgivable sin in the Bible, and it has nothing to do with sexual sin or marital failure. If you are in such a condition right now what should you do?

Seek the Lord's forgiveness. (1 John 1:9).

If you are separated from your spouse, 1 Corinthians 7:11 is the answer.

If you have been violated by your spouse, Ephesians 4:32 opens the door to your future.

1. *Spirit-Filled Life Bible* (Nashville, TN: Thomas Nelson Publishers, 1991), 1389, "Truth-in-Action through Malachi," #2.
2. Ibid., 1385, "Kingdom Dynamics: Malachi 2:14, 15, 16, God Backs Up the Covenant of Marriage."
3. Ibid., 1441, note on Matthew 19:3.
4. Ibid., 1441, "Kingdom Dynamics: Matt. 19:1–9, Divorce Is a Case of a Heart Hardened Toward God."
5. Ibid., 1256, "Introduction to Hosea: Author."
6. Ibid., 1261, Chart: "Israel's Apostasy and Hosea's Marriage."
7. Ibid., 1747, "Truth-in-Action through 1 Corinthians," #1.

Part Two:
The Function
of the
Family

Lesson 5/Role of a Husband

Early in our marriage, we had gone over to spend the afternoon with my husband's family. We were both still in college full-time and working full-time, and a whole afternoon was a lot of precious time! After several hours had gone by, I told my husband that I wanted to go home. He, of course, wanted to stay. One of my new brothers-in-law, in all of his 14-year-old wisdom, said, "You're the boss. Just tell her you're staying. She has to do what you say!"

Thankfully my husband is much more diplomatic than that! But, unfortunately, what my brother-in-law expressed is many people's view of what the role of a husband is: The Boss. But the duty of a husband extends to much, much more: lover, provider, servant, and spiritual covering.

 KINGDOM EXTRA

God designed marriage to illustrate the relationship He intends to have with His people. The husband is to give his wife honor and understanding, protecting her and acknowledging that she is a fully partnered heir of God.

Husband, be kind and gentle with your wife. Honor her as your very best friend. Listen to her and spend time with her. Cherish her and make her feel extremely important. Recognize that not doing so will hinder your prayer life and obstruct answers.[1]

Read the following Scriptures and write down the different roles and responsibilities of a husband that are listed.

Gen. 2:24 (See also Mark 10:7, Prov. 8.)

Prov. 5:18

1 Cor. 7:3, 4

1 Cor. 7:11

Eph. 5:23–29

Col. 3:19

1 Tim. 5:8

Titus 2:6–8 (There is quite a list here, directed at "the young men," not specifically to husbands. However, "the young women" in verse 4 were already wives, so we will assume that the young men were husbands.) Define for yourself what each of these things mean and how they are lived out in our culture today.

1 Pet. 3:7

Read over the list you just made. How are you doing? Write down the areas you are currently doing well on. Then write down the areas you need to improve upon.

KINGDOM EXTRA

A Christian renders service to others *as a way of serving the Lord Christ.* In Colossians 3, the relationship to which this truth is specifically applied is the husband-wife relationship. The role and admonition that God assigns to a husband is meant to be a way of serving his wife. Likewise a distinctive role and direction is given to the wife, according to which she serves her husband.

These roles are not self-chosen, nor are they assigned by the culture in which one lives: they are given by God as a means of manifesting the life of Christ. In this setting the word *submission* acquires its full biblical significance for family life: husband and wife alike are submissive to God in fulfilling the roles that He has given them. In serving each other, husband and wife serve and honor Christ. The word "submit" (Greek *hupotasso*) is formed from *hupo* ("under") and tasso ("to arrange in an orderly manner"). In this context it describes a person who accepts his or her place under God's arranged order. Also, remember that God's directive to submit is not limited to wives. In James 4:7 and Ephesians 5:21 we see the directive applied to every believer—in his or her relationships with others—and with God.[2]

   KINGDOM EXTRA

In Isaiah 54:5, God reveals Himself by the title *husband* to disclose how deeply He loves His people and how effectively He cares for them. In so doing, He unveils an important dimension of human family life with particular reference to husbands: a husband is to love and to take care of his wife and children. God is a *Protector* and a *Provider.* Husbands who open themselves to God's direction will find both the inspiration and the power to be those things for their families, for those attributes of God's being will flow into and fill their lives.[3]

Although the husband is the head of the home and final responsibility for decisions rest with him, his authority flows out of 1) his submission to the Father, and 2) his servant-heart toward his family.

KINGDOM EXTRA

Love is servant spirited. The world-mind will never understand or accept this call. A servant is one who accepts and acknowledges a place beneath those whom he serves, one willing to forsake the systems of social status on our human scale of values. Servants are viewed as performing the unworthy tasks considered beneath those whom they serve. But Jesus says that those who function as His servants—serving the world in His name—will be honored by the heavenly Father. Every true servant will ultimately be honored by the One whom they serve and who has promised them honor for that service!

If we follow and serve our King, in that act of service we are elevated to a place of honor![4]

Read the account of Jesus' healing the centurion's servant (Matt. 8:5–13).

From where did the centurion derive his authority?

From where did Jesus derive His authority?

How is the basis of the husband's authority similar?

The whole issue of submission and authority in the home has been the source of much discussion, controversy, and misuse. In dealing with this subject, however, we must keep several points in mind:

First, God's original intent for the family, as seen in the first couple, was that they would rule over Earth as complete partners: they were one flesh and mutually shared everything in every way. Sin broke that partnership and in the redemptive process, the Lord established the husband as the head of the family. In

Christ, however, the Lord wants to move us back to our position together as "joint heirs" (1 Pet. 3:7). Thus, biblical authority or position is never to be used as an excuse to become some kind of a taskmaster or dictator. As God makes the husband to rule over their home as a king and priest to his God (Rev. 1:6), so He desires for the wife to rise in rulership as queen beside her husband.

Second, the authority of the husband is not to become an excuse for the wife to renege on her responsibilities. The role of a wife will be dealt with in more detail in the next chapter, but let this suffice: some of the worst misuse on the subject of authority has come from women who decide to put all responsibility on their husbands and refuse to use the wisdom and capabilities God gave them. Responding correctly to authority has to do with an attitude of heart and willingness to serve, not in whether or not you may go to the market if your husband hasn't given you specific permission.

 FAITH ALIVE

How is the authority situation in your home? Do you, as the husband, feel that your decisions are respected and observed?

Is your wife continually growing in her own capabilities as joint-ruler with you? Your wife's authority flows out of your authority, just as your authority flows out of God's authority. Are you releasing her to greater levels of ministry as she answers the Lord's call on her life? Do your children respond respectfully and obediently to your authority in the home?

If your authority isn't being honored in your home, perhaps you aren't exercising it in a servant-hearted attitude.

Read John 13:1–17. Notice how Jesus, though He is Savior and Lord, stooped to wash the feet of those He led. What does this tell you about how you are to lead?

 KINGDOM EXTRA

As Jesus took the towel and basin to wash His disciples' feet, His assuming a servant's role exhibits more than humility, but also evidences the psychological security essential to a leader. Jesus' lifestyle and lessons establish the mode for a new kind of leader—the servant-leader (Matt. 20:26–28). The servant leader leads from a position of personal security, that is, knowing who God has made him or her to be, and resting in the peaceful awareness and confidence that God's hand is ordering his or her personal destiny (see this in v. 3, of Jesus). The godly leader is one who stops to help another, who counts others better than himself (Phil. 2:3, 4), who lays down his life for others (John 10:11), who seeks to serve rather than to be served (Luke 22:27). Until a person is ready to wash feet he is not qualified to be a kingdom leader.[5]

Ephesians has much to say about building godly relationships. This is one of the major themes of the New Testament. Our relationships are to be loving, truthful, selfless, and submissive. Simply put, Ephesians exhorts that we relate to others as Jesus relates to the Father and to us. Maintain a *selflessly submissive attitude* in all your family relationships. Understand that this will provide evidence that Christ rules your home.[6]

Look at the following examples of couples in scripture. Some of these examples are positive, some are negative. As you read about each couple, jot down what the husband did right or wrong to contribute to the leadership and atmosphere in his family.

Ahab and Jezebel: 1 Kin. 16:30—22:40

Abigail and Nabal: 1 Sam. 25:2–42

Adam and Eve: Genesis 2:15—3:21

Abraham and Sarah: Genesis 12:10–20; 16:1—18:15; 20:1—21:12

Jacob and Leah/Rachel: Genesis 29:1—30:24

Solomon and bride: The Song of Solomon

Esther and Ahasuerus: The Book of Esther

Ananias and Sapphira: Acts 5:1–11

Mary and Joseph: Matthew 1:18—2:23; Luke 2:1–52

Is there an example here that reflects how you relate to your family? Is it a negative or positive example?

How did this person relate to the Lord in their home? How do you relate to the Lord in your home? Is it similar?

How could this person have improved upon how they related to and led their family?

Would these be good suggestions for you to apply to your family life?

A WORD ABOUT SEXUAL RELATIONS

We've all heard the "not-tonight-I-have-a-headache" jokes. However, over the years, we have noticed in our counseling of couples that the trend seems to be toward husbands saying this to their wives rather than just wives saying this to their husbands. This phenomenon can be blamed on: fear, anger or unforgiveness toward the wife, pornography, masturbation, or adultery. But it has become the new way that men punish their wives—by withholding sex from them and thus excluding them from the "one flesh" covenant and partnership that was established on their wedding day.

Withholding sex can, of course, come from either partner. But whoever it comes from, please know this: it is not scriptural. First Corinthians 7 makes it clear that our bodies are not our own. When we enter into marriage, our bodies become the property of our spouse.

 KINGDOM EXTRA

Christian couples should overcome sexual selfishness and should not deprive one another. If sexual activity is interrupted in marriage, three conditions are necessary: mutual consent; a limited time; spiritual, not selfish, reasons.[7]

 FAITH ALIVE

Write out 1 Corinthians 7:2–5 to get a clear picture of what your sexual responsibility toward your spouse is according to the Bible.

Why is the sexual relationship so important in marriage?

The following questions are to be answered simply between you and the Lord:

Do either you or your spouse use excuses to avoid a sexual relationship? Why?

Do you avoid sex for any of the reasons named above: fear, anger or unforgiveness toward your spouse, pornography, masturbation, adultery?

If so, what do you feel the Lord is calling you to do about it?

Would professional counseling help you and your spouse work through this situation?

How may the Lord be calling you to be a leader in this area of your marriage?

 KINGDOM EXTRA

Sexual intercourse is an intimate expression of affection between a husband and wife. The apostle underscores its importance in marriage by declaring that it is in fact a *duty:* a husband is to be available for his wife at her request, and a wife for her husband at his request.

It is more than an act of biological mating. The Bible calls it a privileged "mystery" by which two people, a man and a woman, become one (Eph. 5:32; see Gen. 2:24). . . .

Marriage is the one and the only place that God has provided for sexual union to take place. In that setting it becomes a powerful symbol of the love between Christ and the church, a pure sharing of joy and delighting one another that is a gift from the hand of God. Outside those boundaries, it eventually becomes destructive.[8]

1. *Spirit-Filled Life Bible* (Nashville, TN: Thomas Nelson Publishers, 1991), 1916, "Truth-in-Action through 1 Peter," #6.

2. Ibid., 1818, "Kingdom Dynamics: Col. 3:18, 19, 23, 24, Husbands and Wives Called to Operate in God's Order."

3. Ibid., 1034, "Kingdom Dynamics: Is. 54:5, The Husband, Protector and Provider."

4. Ibid., 1598, "Kingdom Dynamics: John 13:1–17, Love Is Servant-Spirited."

5. Ibid., 1600, "Kingdom Dynamics: Secure."

6. Ibid., 1798, "Truth-in-Action through Ephesians," #3.

7. Ibid., 1728, note on 1 Corinthians 7:5.

8. Ibid., 1727–1728 "Kingdom Dynamics: 1 Cor. 7:3, 4, Three Sides of Sex: Unity, Symbol of Love, Reserved for Marriage."

Lesson 6/Role of a Wife

Over the years, the concept of submission has been carried to ridiculous lengths: women who have allowed their children to be abused because they were "submitting" to the wishes of their husband; women who wouldn't even go to the market to purchase groceries or do any work around the house without their husband's permission being granted; women who would subject their bodies and minds to horrible sexual perversion because it's what their husband wanted done.

Let's clear the air right now: 1) God does not ask us to put ourselves or our families in dangerous situations to prove we are submitted; 2) He doesn't ask us to turn off our minds, our common sense, or our ability to accomplish tasks and organize our homes to prove we are submitted; and 3) God created sex to be mutually enjoyable and fulfilling to both the husband and the wife. We don't have to subject ourselves to perversion to prove we are submitted.

Let's begin our study by looking at what the biblical definition of submission is.

WORD WEALTH

Submit, *hupotasso, Strong's #5293:* Literally "to stand under." The word suggests subordination, obedience, submission, subservience, subjection. In 1 Corinthians 14:32 it is used to explain that the divine gift of prophetic utterance is put under the control and responsibility of the possessor.[1] *Hupotasso* is also used in Ephesians 5:22 as a command from the Lord to wives in how they obey their husbands. However, please note that the command is not given to the husband to force upon his wife, but rather it is given to the wife to willingly choose and obey the command of the Lord.

KINGDOM EXTRA

Submitting is taking the divinely ordered place in a relationship. Submission can never be required by one human being of another; it can only be given on the basis of trust, that is, to believe God's Word and to be willing to learn to grow in relationships.

Women are never made second to men in general, but the wife is specifically called to accept her husband's leadership.[2]

Look up these other verses on the subject of submission. Write down anything else you learn about how wives are to submit to their husbands.

1 Cor. 11:8–12

Eph. 5:22–24

Col. 3:18

Heb. 13:17

1 Pet. 3:5, 6

1 Pet. 5:5

KINGDOM EXTRA

The specific instructions that the apostle Paul gives to husbands and wives are a glimpse of *the* Bridegroom and Bride—a heavenly model for every marriage on Earth. As a husband, how should I behave toward my wife? Look to Christ, the divine Bridegroom, in His relationship with the Church: love her, sacrifice for her, listen to her concerns, take care of her; be as sensitive to her needs and her hurts as you are to those of your own body.

As a wife, how should I behave toward my husband? Look to the chosen bride, the church, in her relationship with

Christ: respect Him, acknowledge His calling as "head" of the family, respond to His leadership, listen to Him, praise Him, be unified in purpose and will with Him, be a true helper (see Gen. 2:18).

No husband and wife can do this by mere willpower or resolve, but since you (including your marriage) are "His workmanship" ("For by grace you have been saved through faith, and that not of yourselves; it is the gift of God, not of works, lest anyone should boast. For we are His workmanship, created in Christ Jesus for good works, which God prepared beforehand that we should walk in them," Eph. 2:8–10), God will help bring this about.[3]

Of course, being a wife involves much more than simply being submissive. Look up the following verses and write down other roles and responsibilities of the wife that are listed in scripture.

Ruth 2:7

Prov. 31:11–27 (There is quite a list here, and it can be somewhat intimidating! But just remember that this passage is listing all of the things this woman did throughout her life. She didn't do all of these things every day!)

1 Cor. 7:3, 4

1 Cor. 7:10

1 Tim. 3:11

1 Tim. 5:4

Titus 2:4, 5

How are you doing in each of the above listed areas? Are there areas you need to improve upon? List those now to present to the Lord.

KINGDOM EXTRA

The spirit of submission, whereby a woman voluntarily acknowledges her husband's leadership responsibility under God, is an act of faith. The Bible nowhere "submits" or subordinates women to men, generically. But this text calls a woman to submit herself to her husband (Eph. 5:22), and the husband is charged to lovingly give himself to caring for his wife—never exploiting the trust of her submission (v. 7; Eph. 5:25-29). This divinely ordered arrangement is never shown, nor was it ever given, to reduce the potential, purpose, or fulfillment of the woman. Only fallen nature or persistent church traditionalism, finding occasion through "proof-texts" separated from their full biblical context, can make a case for the social exploitation of women or the restriction of women from church ministry.

First Timothy 2:12 and 1 Corinthians 14:34, 35, which disallow a woman's teaching (in an unwelcomed manner), usurping authority, or creating a nuisance by public argument, all relate to the woman's relationship with her husband. (The Greek word for "man" in 1 Timothy 2:12 is *aner,* which is as readily translated "husband" as "man." The context clearly recommends "husband," as does the evidence of the rest of the New Testament related to the viability of a woman's public voice in Christian assemblies.

The Bible's word of wisdom to women seems to be summarized 1 Peter 3:1: counsel given to a woman whose husband is an unbeliever. She is told that her "words" are not her key to success in winning her husband to Christ; but her Christlike, loving spirit is. Similarly, this wisdom would apply to any woman with the potential for a public ministry of leadership in the church. Her place will most likely be given when she is not argumentatively insistent upon it, so much as given to "winning" it by a gracious, loving, servantlike spirit—the same spirit that ought to be evident in the life of a man who would lead.[4]

The servantlike spirit we studied about in the chapter on the role of a husband applies equally to the role of a wife. Take a moment to review the "Kingdom Dynamics" on servanthood listed in that chapter before you go on.

Different women of the Scriptures provide us with servant examples, but Ruth is particularly fitting. Basically, she was a single woman with an elderly roommate, and Ruth was supporting both of them. In the midst of this, the Lord provided her with a husband. So we see Ruth as a single woman and as a married woman. At all times we see a woman whose relationship with the Lord was intact and whose attitudes toward all those around her was in order. We also see a woman who, in spite of hardship, widowhood, and famine, is ready to serve those around her . . . beginning with her family.

 KINGDOM EXTRA

Ruth is replete with principles of righteous and godly relationships. Ruth is a supreme example of someone who prioritizes personal relationships. She exemplifies loyalty, servanthood, diligence, and moral righteousness. Much grief can be avoided when we learn to relate to one another in love and understand what this really implies about our relationships.

Do not make commitments too hastily. Wait until you understand the full implications of any commitment you make to another. Practice loyalty, and understand that a loyal person prioritizes his relationship over personal advantage or comfort. Do not back out of a commitment you make to a friend, even if it means personal sacrifice. Learn servanthood. Know that God calls us to serve those we love. Believe that God will honor those with a servant's heart.[5]

 FAITH ALIVE

Ruth is a very short book of the Bible—only four chapters. Read through it and write down everything that Ruth did to serve Naomi, Boaz, and others around her.

Do you function with a servant heart toward your family like Ruth did?

What lessons can you learn from Ruth that you can apply directly to your own family?

Ruth, in going to Boaz, was also a very bold person. When and where there were conditions in God's law that made provision for her and Naomi, she was bold to accept them. In Ruth we see the fine line between submission and moving in submitted authority.

KINGDOM EXTRA

All rightful authority is derived from God; therefore, to submit to authority honors God. Submission is an act of faith, establishing God as the ultimate authority over the relationship, be it connected with government, church, employment, or home. The higher the authority, the greater the accountability to God.

"**Submit** to and **respect** all authority. **Do not use** your freedom in Christ as an excuse for sin."[6]

FAITH ALIVE

Look up Ephesians 5:33. What is the wife commanded to do?

Every person we know will occasionally do things that disappoint us. Is this a reason to lessen our respect for them?

Sometimes we remember to be courteous and gracious to those outside of our families, but often it's those closest to us that we take our frustrations out on. Is this showing respect to our husbands?

How should we be showing respect to them?

Name three ways that you would like to see the Lord help you improve in this area.

 KINGDOM EXTRA

God rules His people through delegated authority. All authority is from God (see Rom. 13). To distrust those He places over us is to distrust Him. God calls His people to a submissive attitude toward His leaders. He cautions us to be careful how we speak about them.

"**Do not grumble** against spiritual leadership. You thus grumble against the Lord and rebel. . . . **Listen** to those God sends to speak to and lead us. **Do not rebel** against their leadership. To disregard godly leaders is to disregard Him.[7]

1. *Spirit-Filled Life Bible* (Nashville, TN: Thomas Nelson Publishers, 1991), 1742, "Word Wealth: 14:32 subject."
2. Ibid., 1795, notes on Eph. 5:21, 22 and 5:22.
3. Ibid., 1795, "Kingdom Dynamics: Eph. 5:22–33, Christ and the Church Model Husband/Wife Relationships."
4. Ibid., 1911," Kingdom Dynamics: 1 Pet. 3:1, A Word of Wisdom to Wives."
5. Ibid., 394, "Truth-in-Action through Ruth," #1.
6. Ibid., 1916, "Truth-in-Action through 1 Peter," #5.
7. Ibid., 144, "Truth-in-Action through Exodus," #5.

Lesson 7 / The Place of Children in a Family

The world is a "mixed bag of tricks" when it comes to how people view children. On one hand, the United Nations is trying to push through the "Children's Bill of Rights" that exalts children to virtual rulers in the home. On the other hand, the slaughter of children in the womb is practiced throughout our nation as an acceptable form of birth control.

Women who have the economic privilege of staying home to raise their children are viewed as the new status symbol, while Women's Lib views kids as an interruption to life, a hassle, something that holds you back. A generation of junk-food-consuming, latchkey kids are raising themselves. Fathers are often nonexistent except for a monthly support check (if that even comes).

All of this raises questions about how we as believers are supposed to live. Where do children fit into the family order? How are we supposed to view them? What are their requirements and privileges within the family?

Look up and copy Psalm 127:3–5.

What does the psalmist say that is in direct contrast to the world's view of children?

What else does the Bible further say about the blessing of children? (See Is. 8:18.)

Psalm 128:3—"Your children [shall be] like _____."

What do you think "olive plants" represents in this verse?

Prov. 17:6

What place are grandchildren to play in one's old age?

Read 2 Samuel 6:23. How does this verse contrast with the previous verses you have read?

Read all of 2 Samuel 6. What brought about Michal's punishment?

 BEHIND THE SCENES

Verse 6:14 says that David danced. Such rejoicing (literally "spinning around") accompanied all major victories. In every other instance only women are mentioned as dancing, not men and certainly not the king. This accounts for some of Michal's embarrassment (v. 16), although her motive is obviously contempt.

Michal is here described as **Saul's daughter** rather than David's wife. She acts in the pride of her father, not the humility and joy of her husband.[1]

How can Michal's actions and the resultant punishment show us the importance of thankfulness to the Lord?

How could our continued growth in thankfulness affect the way we relate to our children?

Scripture further tells us specifically about Jesus' attitude toward children. In Isaiah 40:11, the prophet tells us about the future reign of the Messiah. What will be His attitude and actions toward children?

Read the following verses to see the fulfillment of Isaiah's prophecy. What was Jesus' attitude toward children?

Matt. 10:42

Matt. 18:2–10; Mk. 9:33–37

Matt. 19:13–15

 FAITH ALIVE

What does Jesus' attitude toward children tell us about how we are to treat children?

List three ways Jesus' treated children that we should apply to our own homes.

1.

2.

3.

KINGDOM EXTRA

Human value cannot be equated with race, wealth, social standing, or educational level. All are significant and valuable in God's order. To regard race, group, or individual as less important than another is sin in view of the fact that Christ died for all people and for each one in particular. At the foot of the Cross we are equal, both in our worth to God (He sent His Son to die for each of us) and in our need to accept His gift of salvation. Let us learn to respect and honor every person and each people regardless of their station or color. Christ said, "Inasmuch as you did it to one of the least of these My brethren, you did it to Me" (Matt. 25:40).[2]

Read the following verses. What do they have to say about showing partiality?

Lev. 19:15

Job 13:10

1 Tim. 5:21

James 2:4

How might this apply to our view of our children?

What do these verses have to say about a parent favoring one of their children over the others?

Scripture gives us an example of a mother who favored one son over another. Who is this mother? (Gen. 25:28)

Read Genesis 25:29–34 and 27:1—28:5. List the ultimate results of Rebekah's favoritism.

(Notice that Rebekah lost Isaac's respect and Jacob's presence anyway.) Did anything good come out of Rebekah's favoritism and subsequent deception? Explain your answer.

   FAITH ALIVE

Jesus, as the Son of God, knew precisely how to keep everything in perfect balance. As sinful humans, we don't always know how to do that, and our "consideration" of our children can get out of balance to the exclusion of the Lord, our spouse, and other responsibilities.

Do you think an attitude of respect and consideration toward children can breed disrespect toward the parent or arrogance on the part of the child? Explain your answer.

How can we balance respect toward our children as people and creations of God with our responsibility to raise them to be people of God? (See Prov. 22:15)

Respect toward one another as creations of the Creator also requires that we recognize and accept the fact that no one is an "accident." Whether or not it appears that way from the human side of things, or whether or not we arrive in a family by birth or adoption, God knew from eternity the birth and future of each one of us. Write out Psalm 68:5, 6.

KINGDOM EXTRA

We sometimes speak about difficult circumstances into which people are born as "an accident of birth." Viewed from a divine perspective, however, our placement in a human family is no accident at all: it is a divine appointment. *"God sets the solitary in families."* Indeed, the protection and care that one receives in a family is so essential to human life that God says He will personally intervene on behalf of widows and orphans who lose the normal protection of a husband and father. When we are tempted to complain about our family, or suppose that our birth-circumstance would be better somewhere else, we need to regain this divine perspective. This is not to become passive or fatalistic about one's situation, nor is it to say this will cause an escape from sorrow or suffering. Nevertheless, we are reminded that the ultimate well-being of our human families rests upon the promise and care of our Father in heaven and that His sovereign and loving purpose will intervene for our benefit.[3]

FAITH ALIVE

How we relate as children to our parents often determines how we relate as parents to our children. Write out below three things that you are thankful for in your parents:

1.

2.

3.

Praise the Lord for your parents!

Write out the three things that are "the biggest sore points" between you and your parents.

1.

2.

3.

Present these to the Lord in prayer and ask Him to make the difference where we can't. Now, having established an atmosphere of appreciation for our parents, let's establish that same atmosphere in regard to our children. Write out three things that you are thankful for in each of your children:

1.

2.

3.

Praise God for your children!

List the three areas that you most fear regarding releasing your children into the Lord's hands.

1.

2.

3.

Once again, present these to the Lord in prayer, asking that He be real in your children's lives, providing protection and drawing them to Himself.

Our rule of the realm God has given us requires that we first have our homes in proper order. Ephesians 5:22—6:3 gives us an "up close and personal" view of how the family structure is to be arranged. Read this passage of Scripture.

List in order the four parts of the family structure.

Who is to be the ultimate head of the family? Who is the God-ordained head here on Earth?

Where does the child fit into the family order?

What are the child's two main responsibilities?

1.

2.

What is the promise connected with this command? (See Ex. 20:12.)

What does Galatians 4:1–7 tell us about the place of children in the family during the years of their minority? (vv. 1, 2)

Why do you think this is so?

What is a child supposed to learn during those years that makes him seem a "slave" rather than a son, but ultimately allows him to step into his complete inheritance as a son?

WORD WEALTH

"Heir," *sunkleronomos* (soong-klay-ron-*om*-oss); *Strong's #4789*: from *sun*, "with," *klero*, "a lot," and *nemomai*, "to possess." The word denotes a joint participant, coheir, fellow heir, one who receives a lot with another.[4]

"Slave," *doulos* (*doo*-los); *Strong's #1401*: from *deo*, "to bind." The word is used for one who is a slave, literally or figuratively, voluntarily or involuntarily, and indicates subjection or subserviency to another.[5]

Read the following scriptures and write down other requirements that are to be placed upon children within the family.

Ex. 20:12

Prov. 1:8; 6:20

Prov. 23:22

1 Tim. 5:4

As parents, we alone carry the responsibility of instilling these values, principles, and ethics into our children's lives. Read Deuteronomy 6:6–9 and list five ways we can accomplish this instruction process in the lives of our children.

Parents aren't the only ones to receive exhortation in the Word on how to live. Children receive specific direction throughout the Book as well. Read the following passages and list ways that Scripture instructs children to relate to their parents and to the world around them. Also list how these scriptures can be applied in your family life.

Ps. 34:11

Prov. 10:1

Prov. 20:11

Eph. 6:1–3; Col. 3:20

Since we are *all* the children of someone, go back over that list of scriptures and write down the ways that these exhortations can be applied to your own life in regard to *your* parents.

 FAITH ALIVE

Compare the verses you've just looked up with Jesus' words in Matthew 18:3?

How can we teach our children to maintain "childlikeness" in their lives?

Are there ways we can instill those lessons by how we maintain "childlikeness" in our lives?

Why do you think Jesus placed such importance on our "becoming as little children"?

How does the Heavenly Father relate to us "as little children"?

How should this affect or change the way you relate to your children?

🔯   KINGDOM EXTRA
_____

Jesus confronts the tendency of humankind to associate authority with an exercise of dominance over others. The dominion or authority in kingdom life God wants to reinstate in us, is for victorious, fruitful living and for the overthrow of hellish powers, not for gaining control of others or for serving our own interests. His call to childlike humility and a servant-like heart (John 13:1–17) establishes the spirit and style by which the authority of the believer is to be exercised as an agent of God's kingdom power. (See Matt. 19:14; Mark 10:14, 15; Luke 18:16, 17.)[6]

In retaining our childlikeness in the kingdom, we must also recognize that throughout our lives we also retain our role as children of our parents. While the way that role is lived out may change over time as we come into our adulthood and our parents grow older, they will always be our parents and we will always be their children. Read the following scriptures and list how we are to relate to our parents as adult children.

Gen. 18:19

Lev. 19:32

Deut. 4:9

Ps. 71:9

Prov. 17:6

Prov. 20:29

1 Tim. 5:1

In what ways is our role toward our parents to change?

In what ways is it to stay the same?

What role are our parents to play in our lives as adults?

Who else are we to treat with the honor and respect due to our parents?

1. *Spirit-Filled Life Bible* (Nashville, TN: Thomas Nelson Publishers, 1991), 450, notes on 2 Samuel 6:14 and 6:16.

2. Ibid., 1897, "Kingdom Dynamics: James 2:1–9, Respect of Persons."

3. Ibid., 809, "Kingdom Dynamics: Ps. 68:5, 6, Divine Appointment Places People in Families."

4. Ibid., 1885, "Word Wealth: 11:9, heirs."

5. James Strong, *Strong's Exhaustive Concordance of the Bible,* (New York: Abingdon Press, 1890), 24, Greek Dictionary #1401.

6. *Spirit-Filled Life Bible,* 1439, "Kingdom Dynamics: Matt. 18:1–4, Childlikeness."

Lesson 8/Biblical Parenting

Parents hold a most unique and challenging role in God's order: we are responsible to raise the next generation of the kingdom of God. This obviously takes us far beyond the mere physical provision of our children's need for food, shelter, and clothing. We have a moral, spiritual, emotional, and intellectual obligation to our children as well.

 FAITH ALIVE

Look up 1 Peter 2:9. Write down what is true of us, and, consequently, true of our children.

Look up Proverbs 22:6. What directive (and promise) does Scripture give to parents to guarantee that their children become the next "chosen generation" of the Lord?

Look up Titus 2:6–8. What are we to teach the younger generation? How does this scripture have an impact on how we live our own lives?

How does 1 Timothy 4:12 tell us we are to teach our children to live?

KINGDOM EXTRA

God holds parents responsible for the upbringing of children—not grandparents, not school, not the state, not youth groups, not peers and friends. Although each of these groups may influence children, the final duty rests with parents, and particularly with the father, whom God has appointed "head" to lead and serve the family. Two things are necessary for the proper teaching of children: a right *attitude* and a right *foundation*. An atmosphere reeking with destructive criticism, condemnation, unrealistic expectations, sarcasm, intimidation, and fear will "provoke a child to wrath." In such an atmosphere, no sound teaching can take place.

The positive alternative would be an atmosphere rich in encouragement, tenderness, patience, listening, affection, firm discipline, and love. In such an atmosphere parents can build into the lives of their children the precious foundation of knowledge of God.[1]

Throughout Scripture, we see how parents influenced their children for righteousness or for evil. Look up the following passages and fill in the chart below:

Scripture	Who are the parents named?	How did they influence their children?	What can we learn from their example?
Gen. 24:1–6 26:1–5			
Ruth 4:13–17			
1 Sam. 2:12–17, 22–25			
1 Kings 1:1–6, 24–27			
2 Chr. 33:21—34:3			

Esth. 5:9–14;
    9:12, 13

2 Tim. 1:3–5

In many cases, we see evil beget evil or good beget good. Yet in some situations we see good beget evil or vice versa. What do you think Eli and David did improperly that allowed their sons to stray toward evil?

What do you think happened in Josiah's life that allowed him to turn toward the Lord in spite of a wicked heritage?

 FAITH ALIVE

What part do you think that heredity has to play in a person's spiritual heritage?

Look up Lamentations 5:7 and Exodus 34:7. What do these verses say about the part our parents play in our spiritual heritage? What kind of spiritual heritage did your parents provide you with?

Whether or not your parents' spiritual input was positive or negative, what does Scripture tell us about our spiritual heritage right now as believers in Jesus Christ?

2 Cor. 5:17

Eph. 4:6

1 Pet. 2:9.

KINGDOM EXTRA

God wants a people who will walk with Him in prayer, march with Him in praise, and thank and worship Him. Note the progression in Peter's description of the people of the New Covenant: 1) *We are a chosen generation*—a people begun with Jesus' choice of the Twelve, who became 120, to whom were added thousands at Pentecost. We are a part of this continually expanding generation, "chosen" when we receive Christ. 2) *We are a royal priesthood.* Under the Old Covenant the priesthood and royalty were separated. We are now—in the Person of our Lord—all "kings and priests to His God" (Rev. 1:6), a worshiping host and a kingly band, prepared for walking with Him in the light or warring beside Him against the hosts of darkness. 3) *We are a holy nation,* composed of Jews and Gentiles—of one blood, from every nation under heaven. 4) *We are His own special people.* God's intention from the time of Abraham has been to call forth a people with a special mission—to proclaim His praise and to propagate His blessing throughout the Earth.[2]

Praise the Lord that upon our receiving of Jesus into our hearts, we inherited a new family, a new Father, a new spiritual heritage!

Look up these verses that also talk about the influence of the righteous on following generations. What does the Lord promise in each verse?

Ps. 37:25, 29

Ps. 102:28

Ps. 112:2

Prov. 20:7

KINGDOM EXTRA

God reveals Himself as a Father who is tender, close to His children, and sensitive to their needs—teaching, encouraging, helping, and healing them. Growing up is not something that He leaves to chance. He is a God who conscientiously *nurtures* His children. God's heart toward His children is tenderly portrayed in the meaning behind Hosea's name. *Hoshea* means "Deliverer" or "Helper." The Hebrew root *yasha* indicates that deliverance or help is freely and openly offered, providing a haven of safety for every child of God.

This is the biblical model for parents: God entrusts children to parents, allowing His own nurturing heart to flow through them to the children.[3]

Look at Hosea 11:1–4 and write down how God nurtured His child, Israel.

Part of having a heart like the Lord's heart requires that we recognize the fact that loving and caring for children honors Him.

KINGDOM EXTRA

God's covenant with Adam and Eve contained two interdependent provisions: *descendants* and *dominion*. Two people alone could not take dominion of the Earth. It would require descendants.

For believers, having children is a response to the command, "Be fruitful and multiply; fill the earth and subdue it" (Gen. 1:28). In Psalm 127:3, children are called "a heritage from the Lord." This means that children belong to God; they are "ours" only in a secondary sense. . . .

When a couple enters into marriage, they make themselves available to love, serve, and sacrifice for the next generation. To love and care for children is one of the principal ways that we honor God and share in building His kingdom.[4]

Once we view parenthood through the heart of God, we then have to get down to the nitty-gritty of practical, everyday-life application. The Bible gives us some very clear directives on what our responsibilities as parents are. Read the following scriptures and write down what the Lord says we are to do as parents.

Prov. 22:6

 KINGDOM EXTRA

Train up has the idea of a parent graciously investing in a child whatever wisdom, love, nurture, and discipline is needed for him to become fully committed to God. It presupposes the emotional and spiritual maturity of the parent to do so. **In the way he should go** is to do the training according to the unique personality, gifts, and aspirations of the child. It also means to train the child to avoid whatever natural tendencies he might have that would prevent total commitment to God (for example, a weak will, a lack of discipline, a susceptibility to depression). Hence, the promise is that proper development insures the child will stay committed to God.[5]

1 Sam. 2:19; 1 Tim. 5:8

2 Sam. 12:16

Is. 38:19

Luke 15:20–24

Eph. 6:4

1 Tim. 3:4

Titus 2:4

Now go back over the list you just prepared and determine whether any of those fall into the three major areas of parental responsibility: moral, intellectual, or spiritual.

Before we go on and for the purpose of our study, let's agree on definitions for these three words. First, "intellect" can be defined as the ability to reason, to understand, to discern differences. "Moral" has to do with being able to distinguish between right and wrong in behavior or character. *Webster's* defines "spirit" as "the life principle, especially in man, originally regarded as inherent in the breath or as infused by a deity; the thinking, motivating, feeling part of man, often as distinguished from the body."[6]

The words used for "spirit" in the Bible define it even further for us. In Hebrew, the word is *ruach,* meaning spirit, wind, or breath. In the New Testament, the Greek word *pneuma* carries a similar meaning. In Genesis 6:17, "the *ruach* of life" is translated "the breath of life." Generally *ruach* is translated "spirit," whether concerning the human spirit, a distressing spirit (1 Sam. 16:23), or the Spirit of God.[7] *Pneuma* is that part of a person capable of responding to God.[8]

Ephesians 5:1–21 gives us an outline to follow in providing our children with a sound moral, spiritual, and intellectual basis for life. Approaching the raising of our children, however, requires strength of character on our part, determination, and, above all, consistency in every area of our lives and in how we administer God's standards in our homes.

Our moral obligation can be fulfilled as we teach our children the truths found in Ephesians 5:1–7. Look up these verses and list the things we are to teach our children to follow and avoid.

FAITH ALIVE

Ephesians 5:1 says that we are to imitate God "as dear children." This assumes that our children are also trying to imitate their parents—us! Based on this passage, what might you need to change in your life to be an example worthy of being imitated?

Doubtless there will be times that each of us will be misunderstood by our children as we seek to live out the will of God in raising them. But take heart. Scripture even gives us a guideline to follow for the years of the minority of our children. Read Galatians 4:1, 2. What light does it shed on how our children are to be dealt with in their younger years?

How can these verses be lived out in an atmosphere of love?

What do you think might be the benefits for a child of being treated as a "servant" in the home (as described in the Galatians passage) rather than as an peer?

Look up Mark 10:43, 44. How might these verses tie in to the Galatians verses? How might learning to "be a servant" in their younger years help our children's ability to "be great" in their adulthood?

Look up these other verses that tell other aspects of God's moral standard. Write down what we are to learn.

Mic. 6:8

James 2:9

FAITH ALIVE

Matt. 5:8; 1 John. 3:3

John 4:23, 24; 15:26

Stop right now and ask the Lord to show you how you are to apply His moral standards to your home life in a firm, yet nonjudgmental, loving atmosphere.

Recently, in a conversation with my teenage son, I was struck again with the importance and priority of my spiritual task as a parent. As we talked, I shared with him how, as concerned as I was with his physical well-being, his emotional wholeness, his grades, his sports, everything about his life, I was more concerned about his soul—because that's the only part of him that will endure for eternity. For the first time, he began to see how everything else pales in comparison to that aspect of our lives.

Ephesians 5:8–14 tells us about how we can meet our spiritual responsibility. Read this passage and list the things that the Lord says are to be part of a godly life.

Instilling these truths into our children's hearts is a number-one, full-time parenting priority, because the greatest need any of us ever have is for salvation. This need applies equally to our children.

KINGDOM EXTRA

The value of the human being can be inferred from the price paid to redeem man (John 3:16; 1 Cor. 6:20). God the Son, the Divine One through whom the worlds were created, became flesh and died for the sins of humanity. That He willingly shed His blood and died for us reveals not only the value of the human personality, but also the importance of salvation. Through Christ, believers are forgiven, reckoned to be righteous, and by new birth are renewed in the image of

God. Fallen men and women can only produce the works of the flesh. Only the Spirit, by the new birth, can renew and recover that which was destroyed by the Fall (John 3:5, 6). To reach highest human potential, to have abundant life, one must accept Jesus Christ by faith.[9]

To communicate fully the importance of the spiritual dimension of our lives and live it to its ultimate fullness, we must be willing to acknowledge that the spiritual/invisible part of our lives is as real—maybe even more real—than the physical/tangible part of our lives. Look up these verses to see what the Bible has to say about living our lives in the invisible realm.

Rom. 1:20

2 Cor. 4:18

Col. 1:15, 16

Heb. 11:27

Seeing into the invisible realm, through the power of the Holy Spirit, is what gives us the insight to deal with each of our children at their own level of need, understanding, and maturity level, impacting every onslaught Satan would attempt to make in their lives. And as we teach them these principles of life, they can begin to apply them to their own lives so when they leave our care, their spiritual growth doesn't come to a standstill.

We begin the spiritual influence in our children's lives when they are infants by presenting them in dedication to the Lord. Read about the dedications of Samuel and Jesus. What lessons can you draw from these examples? Is dedication a one-time event or is there an application we can make every day?

1 Sam. 1:19–28

Luke 2:22–24

Read the following verses and list other spiritual principles that we are to instill into our children.

Ps. 31:23

Ps. 138:2

Prov. 16:20

Eph. 6:1

James 4:10

 FAITH ALIVE

How do you think that requiring our children to respond with these traits to us as their parents will help them respond to the Lord as their heavenly Father as they reach maturity? If we are going to require our children to respond with these traits to us, explain the importance of developing these traits in our own lives.

Now turn to Ephesians 5:15–21 as we explore how to live out our intellectual duty in raising our children. We've already defined "intellect" as the ability to reason and discern. This pulls our parenting responsibility out from merely getting our children to respond by their actions to helping them develop into thinking, reasoning people who can make wise choices based on God's Word.

Read Ephesians 5:15–21 and list how the Lord tells us to walk in wisdom.

"Do not be unwise," verse 17 exhorts us, "but understand. . . ." Proverbs 1:20—4:27 describes wisdom as a discerning and beautiful woman we are to embrace and cling to throughout our lives. Take time to read this extended passage of scripture soon, but for our purposes right here, read 4:7–13 and list the ways wisdom exalts a person.

Read these other verses and list the ways we are to relate to the Lord (and teach our children to relate to Him) from an intellectual point of view.

Ps. 78:5–8

Ps. 119:15

Prov. 9:10

2 Tim. 3:15

James 1:5

All of this can seem a daunting task to even the most stouthearted parent! But the Lord has not left us without encouragement. Read the following verses and list how the Lord has promised to help us accomplish what He has set before us.

Deut. 33:27

Ps. 18:35

Is. 41:10

Is. 46:4

1. *Spirit-Filled Life Bible* (Nashville, TN: Thomas Nelson Publishers, 1991), 1796, "Kingdom Dynamics: Eph. 6:4, Parents Responsible to Raise Children."
2. Ibid., 1910, "Kingdom Dynamics: 1 Pet. 2:9, Worshipful Walk with God."
3. Ibid., 1269, "Kingdom Dynamics: Hosea 11:1, 3, 4, God's Nurturing Heart in Parents Flows to Children."
4. Ibid., 866, "Kingdom Dynamics: Ps. 127:3–5, Loving and Caring for Children Honors God."
5. Ibid., 912, note on 22:6
6. *Webster's New World Dictionary of the American Language* (New York: World Publishing Co., 1970) 732, "intellect."
7. *Spirit-Filled Life Bible*, 474, "Word Wealth: 2 Sam. 23:2 Spirit."
8. Ibid., 1697, "Word Wealth: Romans 7:6 Spirit."
9. Ibid., 1908, "Kingdom Dynamics: 1 Pet. 1:18, 19, Man's Greatest Need Is for Salvation."

Lesson 9/ *The Way of Family Discipline*

In the last chapter, we saw our responsibility to raise our children in the ways of the Lord. In this chapter we will be looking at our responsibility as parents to discipline our children.

Here again the world's view is drastically different from God's. While the world claims that indulgence and so-called "freedom" are the way to raise children, God warns of dire consequences if we do not rule within His laws and provide our children with uncompromising boundaries. He further teaches us that when these boundaries are crossed, we as parents are required to exercise firm discipline accompanied by punishment when appropriate.

 KINGDOM EXTRA

Discipline is the other side of teaching. A child with a teachable spirit will still need thorough explanation, much patience, opportunity to try and experiment, including the right to fail and to learn by failure. A child, however, who is caught up in willful disobedience (Prov. 29:15), rebellion (1 Sam. 15:23), or stubborn foolishness (Prov. 22:15), closes off effective teaching and disrupts the harmony of the family. God's answer to this is firm and loving discipline.

The Bible makes a clear distinction between discipline and physical abuse. Discipline may be painful but not injurious. We are never to inflict harm on a child (Prov. 23:13), but at times pain may be a part of effective correction. God describes Himself as a strict disciplinarian. Although He always disciplines us out of love and for our own benefit, His correction may cause us pain (Heb. 12:5–11). Likewise, God requires that parents properly correct their children. Even a child's eternal destiny can hinge upon the godly discipline provided by parents (Prov. 23:14).[1]

Look up the following verses and respond as directed. Write down the different ways the Lord directs us to discipline our children.

Deut. 8:5, 6

Prov. 3:11, 12

Rev. 3:19

What is God's purpose in chastening His people? How does discipline reinforce our love for our children?

Ps. 94:12

What place does teaching have in disciplining our children?

Jer. 10:24

Justice carries with it the idea of fairness, equity, and truth. How are these principles supposed to guide how we discipline?

1 Cor. 4:14

Rom. 15:14

Define "admonish." Where does this fit into your concept of discipline?

Eph. 6:4

The world understands corporal discipline only from the standpoint of someone functioning in uncontrolled rage. Explain how in the Lord, we can discipline and punish our children without acting in anger ourselves or driving our children to anger in response.

List the three different types of people described in 1 Thessalonians 5:14. Can children fall into any or all of these three categories? Does Scripture recommend the same type of discipline for each? What does this teach us about how we deal with our children?

Explain the wisdom of the Lord's directive that we discipline promptly.

Prov. 10:13

Prov. 13:24

Prov. 19:18

Prov. 22:15

Prov. 23:13, 14

KINGDOM EXTRA

Beat him with a rod means to spank a child with one's hand or an instrument of sufficient strength so as to cause pain but not injury. The Bible teaches that spanking is to stem from an attitude of love and patience (Heb. 12:3–6), is necessary because of Adamic foolishness in children (Prov. 22:15), can come too late in a child's life to be effective (19:18), and is a necessary part of nurturing spiritual development (v. 14).[2]

Prov. 29:15

List three ways that corporal discipline would instill wisdom in a child.

CONSEQUENCES OF NOT REQUIRING DISCIPLINE

Scripture gives warning that awful consequences will come of refusing to administer proper discipline. Refusing to administer proper discipline can come about in a number of ways:

1. We can do nothing—ignoring the violation.
2. We can overreact—dispensing a punishment that doesn't fit the offense.
3. We can underreact—teaching our children that they can "get off easy."
4. We can threaten—undermining the authority of our words in our children's lives.
5. We can excuse—explaining away wrong behavior.
6. We can punish without proper explanation—creating fear and confusion.

In all of these instances, children learn to despise discipline, to pay no attention to it, to treat it as a dispensable part of their lives and to hold in contempt any authority who would attempt to administer righteous correction. This gives place to attitudes in their lives of rebellion, disrespect, and foolishness. Scripture gives us several instances where correction was either not applied or was out-and-out rejected. Look up these verses to write down the consequences of allowing our children to despise discipline.

1 Sam. 3:13

1 Sam. 8:3

1 Kin. 1:6

Jer. 5:3

Zeph. 3:7

The prophetic books of the Old Testament are a recounting of what was to happen to Israel, the Lord's child, as a result of their rebellion. Their repeated refusal to respond to gentle discipline brought a much harsher punishment upon them. In the manner He dealt with His people, Israel, the Lord has shown us there are levels of discipline.

Read Hebrews 12:5–13 and write down the different words used for discipline. According to this passage, what do you think is the purpose of discipline?

Compare this passage to Proverbs 3:11, 12. Are there any different words used for discipline here?

From these texts, we can see that there are different types of discipline. One type is simple instruction of a child. Another kind is a verbal rebuke, a caution or warning. Finally there is a place for physical discipline for a child who persists in disobedience after instruction and rebuke have taken place.

At this point our beliefs and the application of them widely diverge from the world. Here we must take a look at how we physically discipline our children. As we've already seen, God does not "spank" us for everything, and neither should we spank for every infraction. Less serious violations can be dealt with "physically" in a variety of ways. "Time out" in the corner, having a privilege taken away, or being assigned extra chores are other ways of physically dealing with a situation (since these punishments can't rightly be called instruction or rebuke), without having to resort to spanking for everything. While there is a place for spanking, it weakens in impact if we use it for everything.

Let this not sound as though the "application of the rod" is being discouraged. Scripture also makes clear that spanking is an act of obedience, faith, and trust on our part. We obey

God's Word, we believe His promises, and we trust that He will work in our children, bringing wisdom and deliverance to their lives.

 FAITH ALIVE

Look up, copy, and memorize Proverbs 23:14.

How have you dealt with physical discipline in your home?

Do you feel that you've spanked too much or too little?

How can you remedy that situation?

What are some ways you can apply physical discipline besides spanking?

Look up the following verses to see what are the results of our obedience.

Deut. 5:29

Job 36:11

Prov. 15:20

Prov. 23:24

Heb 12:11

James 1:25

Read Deuteronomy 7:12–26 and 28:1–14 and list all of the ways the Lord wants to bless those who serve Him and raise their children to follow His ways.

1. *Spirit-Filled Life Bible* (Nashville, TN: Thomas Nelson Publishers, 1991), 901, "Kingdom Dynamics: Prov. 13:24, Corrective Discipline for the Rebellious."

2. Ibid., pg. 913, note on 23:13, 14.

Part Three:
The Fulfillment
of the
Family

Lesson 10/Families Filled with Love

Love is the foundation, the motivation, and the fundamental principle behind everything that has to do with the kingdom of God. "For God so loved the world," Jesus declared. "The greatest of these is love," the apostle wrote. "They will know you are Mine, if you love one another," our Savior further announced.

This is no less true in our families. In fact, in a turbulent culture filled with divorce, violence, abuse, drugs, lawlessness, and disorder, the impact of God's love in our homes becomes indispensable if we are going to order our homes after God's commands.

 KINGDOM EXTRA

John 15:12, 13 summarizes the entire duty and direction of the disciple of Jesus. The direct simplicity of this statement establishes the priority and the pathway we are to pursue. 1) Our priority is to love one another. 2) Our pathway is to love as Christ loved us, "laying down His life." Who can measure this love? Christ gave up the comforts, joys, and adoration of heaven to be sullied by the soil of Earth and to carry the sins of sinners. His bearing of agonizing pain through beatings, nails in His hands, the spear in His side, the thorns on His head, all exemplify the measure of His love. We find His love, but we also see His manner of loving and are called to bear with others' sins, with inflicted pain, with stabbing, cruel remarks and treatment. Impossible? Yes, to human nature; but as new temples of the Holy Spirit, who has poured out the love of God into our hearts, we can ask for and receive the grace and guidance to love as Jesus loved.[1]

Look up these foundational verses about God's love in our lives and write down how they are to impact our family life.

John 14:23

Rom. 8:35

Rom. 12:10

   **WORD WEALTH**

Brotherly love, *philadelphia* (*Strong's #5360*): From *phileo,* "to love," and *adelphos,* "brother." The word denotes the love of brothers, fraternal affection. In the New Testament it describes the love Christians have for other Christians.[2]

Love, *phileo* (*Strong's #5368*) literally means to be fond of, care for affectionately, cherish, take pleasure in, have personal attachment for. In John 21:15–19, Jesus asked Peter twice if he had *agape* love. Peter answered with *phileo,* which at that moment was all he had to give. Later, when the Holy Spirit imparted to him the fuller understanding of *agape* love, Peter used the *agape/agapao* words nine times in his writings.[3]

Rom. 13:8

Gal. 5:13, 14

Phil. 1:9

Col. 2:2

1 Thess. 4:9

Write down three ways that God teaches us to love one another.

1 John 3:16

1 John 3:18

WORD WEALTH

Love, *agape (Strong's #26)*: A word to which Christianity gave new meaning. Outside of the New Testament, it rarely occurs in existing Greek manuscripts of the period. *Agape* denotes an undefeatable benevolence and unconquerable goodwill that always seeks the highest good of the other person, no matter what he does. It is the self-giving love that gives freely without asking anything in return, and does not consider the worth of its object. *Agape* is more a love by choice than *philos,* which is love by chance; and it refers to the will rather than the emotion. *Agape* describes the unconditional love God has for the world.[4]

Thus we see that while God's love is foundational in our homes, it is also based on our will. The media have made it acceptable for couples being married to intone the superficial words, "For as long as we both shall *love,*" assuming that "love" is merely a passing emotion. "As long as it lasts—great! But as soon as it's gone, I'm out the door looking for bigger and better game." There is little recognition that true love— God's kind of love—steps beyond passion to commitment and confidence that we can live out God's will together.

Love is a choice! Thus God *commands* us to love. Look up the following verses and write down who and what God commands us to love.

Lev. 19:18

Lev. 19:34

Deut. 6:5

Ps. 119:97

Prov. 4:5, 6

Amos 5:15

Mic. 6:8

Zech. 8:17, 19

Matt. 5:44

John 13:34

Eph. 5:25

2 Tim. 4:8

Titus 2:4

1 Pet. 1:7, 8

What or how are we commanded not to love?

Prov. 20:13

1 Tim. 6:10

1 John 2:15

1 John 3:18

 KINGDOM EXTRA

That Christ would command us to love indicates that love is not just a feeling or a preference; it is what one does and how he relates to others—a decision, a commitment, or a way of behaving. Jesus states that the world will know that we are His disciples if we behave lovingly toward one another. Schisms, disputes, unkind criticisms, and defamation of character are contrary to the spirit of Christ. His love was sacrificial. It was unconditional love. His love is constant and self-sustaining. His love provides for the best interests of the beloved, and He commands that we should love one another as He has loved us.[5]

 FAITH ALIVE

Look at the following verses to see how unconditional love was lived out in the life of Jesus; then answer the questions that follow.

Matt. 9:36

Matt. 19:13, 14

Mark 2:16, 17

Luke 4:40

Luke 22:42

John 8:10, 11

John 11:35, 36

From these few examples, we see that Jesus' love was uncompromising without being judgmental, willing to relinquish comfort and convenience for the sake of others, always accepting and available. What areas in your family life need to be affected by this kind of selfless love?

How can the examples above from the life of Jesus teach you how to show more love to those in your family?

Can you think of any other examples from Jesus' life that would apply to your situation? Write them down.

Knowing your personality, what will be the greatest drawback to seeing these changes come about?

Before you present these things to the Lord, look up Matthew 7:7, 8 and write it down.

What does the Lord say He will do for anyone who asks? Now present your situation to the Lord, believing that He will strengthen and equip you to show His love in your home.

 KINGDOM EXTRA

In 1 John, we are given steps to sharing the love of God. God revealed Himself to us through Jesus Christ, that we might have the light of life within by the presence of the Holy Spirit. Our mission is to let the light abide within us and shine forth to the glory of God. This produces light in the lives of others, extending the fellowship of God. Love for others is the sure sign that God lives in us and that we are in the fellowship of His love.

Be full of joy. Have fellowship with God and his people (1 John 1:3, 4). Let God's Word live in you, so that you can live in God. Have eternal life! (2:24, 25). Understand that righteousness manifests itself in righteous behavior. Practice righteousness. Love your brother (3:7–15). Understand that fear shows an absence of love. Know that Christ's presence always results in love (4:7–19).[6]

Look up the following verses and write down how God's presence and His love are coupled together in our lives.

John 15:9

Rom. 5:8

1 Cor. 16:23, 24

Gal. 5:22

Eph. 3:19

Eph. 5:2

2 Thess. 3:5

1 Tim. 1:14

1 John 4:7

God's presence in our lives is a prerequisite to having His love, and the closer we come to Him, the closer we get and the more loving we can be to those around us. Yet Psalm 15 teaches us that the converse is also true: to draw closer to God, we must love others.

 KINGDOM EXTRA

In Psalm 15, David is asking God the necessary qualifications to abide in His tabernacle (v. 1). God's reply emphasizes that to "abide" in God's presence and purpose first requires a will to exhibit a strong relationship with others. To expect to have a strong relationship with God, determine to conduct life in right relationship with others! God tells David 1) to speak kindly of his neighbors; 2) never to gossip or say anything to destroy another's reputation; 3) to do nothing to hurt another person in *any* way. 4) Finally, God warns David not to "reproach" his neighbor. "Reproach" (Hebrew *cherpah*) means "blame, discredit, disgrace, or shame." If the Old Testament teaches that one desiring to get closer to God must prioritize love toward others, the New Testament commandment "Love your neighbor as yourself (Rom. 13:9) is surely vital to our relationship with the heavenly Father today.[7]

 FAITH ALIVE

Look at items one through four in the Kingdom Extra above. Write down how each of these can be applied within your family relationships.

1. Speak kindly

2. Don't spread rumors

3. Don't inflict hurt of any kind

4. Don't accuse, embarrass, discount, or disgrace

First Corinthians gives us an even more detailed list of what the actions and responses of love are to be. Turn to 1 Corinthians 13:4–8 and write down the sixteen actions of love that Paul lists and what they mean. Example: "believes all things" (v. 7); Love always believes the best.

Explain in your own words the meaning of verses 1–3, and the necessity of having a loving attitude behind our actions.

Verses 9–12 explain to us that we live in an imperfect age where the things of God are revealed to us only in part. But when we enter eternity, we will see clearly and know completely. What are the three virtues that the Lord has given us to navigate our time here on Earth? (See v. 13.)

What is the greatest of these? Why do you think it is the greatest?

 KINGDOM EXTRA

The virtues of faith, hope, and love are necessary in this age; but in the age to come, faith will give way to sight (2 Cor. 5:7), and hope will turn into experience (Rom. 8:24). Love alone is eternal, for God is love (1 John 4:8).[8]

The fact that God is love becomes a kingdom principle that is at the heart of all our relationships.

 KINGDOM EXTRA

Jesus Christ gave a law that is so profound it should be adopted by every society. It is the law of reciprocity. I use the term "law" because it is a universal principle: "Whatever you want men to do to you, do also to them" (Matt. 7:12). How profound an effect this "Golden Rule" would have if applied at every level in our world!

You would not want a neighbor to steal your tools, so do not take his. You would not like to be struck by a reckless driver, so do not drive recklessly. You would want a helping hand in time of need, so help others in need. In industry, we would not want the person upstream from us polluting the river, so we should not do it to the person downstream from us. We would not want to breathe chemically polluted air, so we should not pollute someone else's air. In the workplace, we would not want to be oppressed, so we should not oppress our employees. If applied, this kingdom law would remove the need for armies, jails, and prisons; problems would be relieved, the burden of government reduced and the productive energies of all the people released. "Do unto others as you would have them do unto you," if put into practice, would revolutionize our society. This is the kingdom foundation for all social relationships.[9]

Look up the following verses to see what the Lord promises to do in our relationships—even in our relationship to Him!

Mal. 4:6

John 13:35

Rom. 8:15

Rom. 12:9

Gal. 4:6

Jude 20, 21

Now turn to 2 Peter 1:5–8 to see the steps we must take to see love birthed in our lives. Fill in the flow chart below to see how we progress and grow in the things of the Lord.

Begin with:

add to that:

add to that:

add to that:

add to that:

add to that:

add to that:

the final result will be:

  KINGDOM EXTRA

Peter gives us a progressive list of Christian virtues that, when established in our lives, will cause us to be fruitful in the very knowledge of God. The life that comes from the knowledge of God can produce only good in its response to others. To fail to grow in Christ results in an inability to perceive the blessings received in initial salvation so that our identification with Jesus is forgotten or ignored.

Recognize that an effective and productive life results from sanctification (character transformation) that begins with faith and results in love.[10]

1. *Spirit-Filled Life Bible* (Nashville, TN: Thomas Nelson Publishers, 1991), 1604, "Kingdom Dynamics: John 15:12, 13, The Priority and Pathway of Brotherly Love."

2. Ibid., 1889, "Word Wealth: 13:1 *brotherly love*."

3. Ibid., 1615, "Word Wealth: 21:15 *love*."

4. Ibid., 1694, "Word Wealth: 5:5 *love*."

5. Ibid., 1601, "Kingdom Dynamics: John 13:34, 35, Love—The Testing of Discipleship."

6. Ibid., 1935, "Truth-in-Action through 1 John," #1.

7. Ibid., 763, "Kingdom Dynamics: Ps. 15:3, To Get Closer to God, Love Others."

8. Ibid., 1740, note on 1 Cor. 13:13.

9. Ibid., 2008, "Spiritual Answers to Hard Questions, #33."

10. Ibid., 1923, "Truth-in-Action through 2 Peter," #2.

Lesson 11 Forgiveness—
Love in Action

Our salvation has been obtained for us through God's abundant love and His merciful forgiveness. It is the basis of our relationship with Him, and therefore should come as no surprise that it is the basis of our relationship with those around us.

Let's look at some of the things Jesus had to say about forgiveness. As you look up these verses, think about what the implications are for us: 1) in our forgiveness received from the Father, and 2) in our forgiveness given to those around us. Write down your observations.

Matt. 6:12–15

Matt. 9:2–6

Matt. 18:21–22

Mark 11:25–26

Luke 6:37

Luke 7:47

Luke 17:3, 4

The Gospel of John doesn't specifically use the word "forgive," however we see this same forgiving attitude lived out in Jesus' ministry as He speaks with individual people. Look at the following episodes and write down what Jesus' attitude toward these people was and how He ministered forgiveness to them.

3:1–21 (note vv. 16–17)

4:5–26

5:1–15

8:3–12

 KINGDOM EXTRA

A major emphasis of Jesus' teaching is how to build and maintain right relationships with God and man. He views these relationships as neither unimportant nor extraneous, but as the essence of which life is made. Knowing God is our highest priority, but this pursuit should not replace or diminish our interpersonal relationships with others. Rather, our personal interaction with God should produce within us the qualities of character that build and sustain all our relationships.

Practice instant reconciliation. Understand that conflicts cause much greater damage to relationships when left unresolved. Understand that God forgives us our sins as we forgive others who have sinned against us. Adopt the forgiveness of others into your prayer life as a daily discipline. Correct your faults and solve your own problems before attempting to correct faults or problems in others. Let any judgmental attitude in yourself signal the need to examine yourself for things that bother you about others.[1]

Forgiveness as practiced within the family unit goes in all directions: parent to child, child to parent, spouse to spouse. And it is our attitude toward God that ultimately determines our attitudes toward one another. If we truly recognize how great our salvation and God's forgiveness are in our thankfulness to the Father, we can do nothing less than extend that same forgiveness and greatness of heart to everyone around us.

KINGDOM EXTRA

Our attitudes toward our mates are governed by our attitudes toward God. A husband may fall short of a wife's expectations and of God's ideal for a husband. Nevertheless, she seeks in every way to be a good wife, modeling her behavior on Christ, who obeyed and trusted the Father even when His own people rejected Him (John 1:11). Or, a wife may disappoint her husband, disregard his authority, or withhold her respect. Nevertheless, a husband honors his wife, cares for her, and prays for her, modeling his behavior on the Father, who "knows our frame" (Ps. 103:14).[2]

 FAITH ALIVE

Are there areas where you have been disappointed by a spouse or child? What are they?

Have you allowed any of these disappointments to turn into bitterness and unforgiveness in your soul? How has it affected your behavior toward this person?

Has harboring unforgiveness affected your relationship with the Lord?

Based on the scriptures we've looked at so far, what is the Lord calling you to do with these disappointments?

In your heart?

In your actions?

In your relationship with Him?

KINGDOM EXTRA

In Matthew 18:18–35, Jesus' prefacing words make this "kingdom" parable of the unforgiving servant especially crucial. The human capacity to forget God's gracious gift of forgiveness and allow smallness of soul to breed unforgiveness is soberingly warned against. 1) Jesus showed how unforgiveness can restrict what God would do in others. (Note: the jailed fellow-servant is still in prison at the story's end, revealing the power of unforgiveness to "bind" circumstances to an undesirable level of perpetual problem.) 2) Jesus teaches how the spirit of unforgiveness (the torturers, literally "bill collectors") exacts its toll on our bodies, minds, and emotions. Finally, every "kingdom" person is advised to sustain a forgiving heart toward all other persons. Kingdom privileges and power must not be mishandled. The "binding" power of unforgiveness is potentially dangerous to any of us.

Matthew 18:18, 19 is frequently quoted to assert the believer's authority in prayer. But the power to "bind and loose" is quickly shown to be as much of a liability as an asset if unforgiveness remains in the people of God's kingdom.[3]

FAITH ALIVE

We've already looked at the words of Jesus on forgiveness, and He makes it clear that we have a responsibility to forgive one another, if for no other reason that we will be forgiven by the Father. In light of the above "Kingdom Dynamic," answer the following questions:

How can unforgiveness "bind up" the unforgiven person?

How can it "bind up" you?

Name before the Lord any known areas of unforgiveness and related bondage. Ask Him to free you and grow your heart to love and forgive the people who have hurt you.

At times, we have all looked at the issue of forgiveness and thought, *Easier said than done.* Other times we've thought, *But you don't know what they did. They hurt me so deeply.* Sometimes forgiveness has come easily, and at other times, feeling that we've fully forgiven someone has taken weeks. But the Lord never allows us to use time, hurt, or difficulty as an excuse to avoid forgiving anyone. He calls us to keep our hearts free and clear before Him. Our ultimate responsibility is between us and Him; and out of that responsibility flows our responsibility to others. Thus, forgiveness becomes an act of faith. We forgive because we have been forgiven, and because we believe that through forgiveness ultimate freedom will come.

Perhaps there are no more difficult and demanding relationships in which to maintain a free and forgiving atmosphere than within our families. We're more likely to offend, wound, or become angry with those we spend the most time with and are closest to—both relationally and physically. But forgiveness can work miracles in families!

 KINGDOM EXTRA

Through the tragic story of Hosea and Gomer, God reveals *both* the depth and power 1) of His love for Israel and 2) of the marriage bond. God describes His suffering the pain and humiliation of Israel's unfaithfulness; and in obedience to God, Hosea suffers the same pain and humiliation of his own wife's unfaithfulness. But God shows him how the marriage can be saved: through *suffering* and *forgiveness.*

This is one of the most profound revelations about marriage found anywhere in Scripture. Successful marriage is not a business of perfect people living perfectly by perfect principles. Rather, marriage is a state in which very imperfect people often hurt and humiliate one another, yet find the grace to extend forgiveness to one another, and so allow the redemptive power of God to transform their marriage.[4]

FAITH ALIVE

Can you think of a situation where a loving act of forgiveness cleared the air and brought healing to a relationship? Was this situation preceded by emotional suffering such as Hosea experienced?

A lot is said in our society today to the effect that no one should ever have to stay in a relationship (such as Hosea's) that inflicts any kind of emotional suffering. What do you think about that?

Do you think God experienced emotional suffering over our unforgiven state when we strayed from Him?

How should God's attitude toward us before we were forgiven affect our attitudes toward others who have hurt us?

KINGDOM EXTRA

It has been said that most teaching on family life is simply an application of what it means to live as a Christian. Romans 15:5–7 is directed to the Christian community at large, yet they present a beautiful and fitting description of Christian marriage.

The key word is "receive" (Greek *proslambano*), which means "to take to oneself." Its root indicates strong action toward us—that in Christ, God literally came to us and *took hold of us* "while we were still sinners" (5:8). By that act of acceptance He released the grace of God and set in motion the powers of redemption.

When that power is allowed to work in a family, it will transform the lives of two imperfect people into one life, lived to the praise of God's glory. Therefore, the Lord sets this word like a banner over marriage from the first day until the last, "Receive one another, just as Christ also received us, to the glory of God."[5]

Oftentimes we would not even find the need for forgiving and of asking for forgiveness if we put a little more time, energy, courtesy, and effort into maintaining good relationships with those closest to us. We sometimes take advantage of the people we see most often, thinking that we can "let our hair down" with them and let them see our "bad side." I remember one particularly embarrassing moment with my husband when, in the middle of an argument, I smarted off, "I don't have to be nice to you! You're my husband!" Unfortunately, that's exactly how many people treat their families all the time. But as with all relationships, family relationships require some work on our part!

Can you think of any situations where you could have avoided hurt feelings with members of your family if you had used a little courtesy and wisdom?

What could you have done differently?

What would you think are the three most important things to remember in relating to our families in order to avoid misunderstanding and injured feelings?

Probably what gets us into the most trouble is what we say!

 KINGDOM EXTRA

Few sins exist that do not somehow involve the tongue. Righteous speech results from discipline and choice. Too easily do we speak too much, too hastily, and too freely. Choosing to speak much less and more carefully will result in less sinning.

Choose to speak only that which is righteous. Commit yourself to godly conversation. Do not grumble and complain when in distress or trouble. Cry out to God. Trust that He will hear and answer. Guard carefully your speech. Know that righteous speech carries with it the promise of long life.[6]

   KINGDOM EXTRA

Proper speech is crucial to effective Christian living. Proverbs points out that life and death are in the power of the tongue. How important it is for us to realize that our speech can be spiritually motivated.

Be careful how you speak and what you say. Reject evil attitudes; and develop compassionate, forgiving attitudes toward others. Avoid and reject any impure or immoral speech or behavior. Be certain that it contradicts your profession of faith in Christ.[7]

Bridle your tongue! Monitoring every word we speak may seem cumbersome at first, but it will serve to advance righteousness. Speak well of others. Criticism, slander, backbiting, and gossip are "bitter waters," which issue out of demonic worldly wisdom.[8]

   FAITH ALIVE

We all have areas of being tempted to say things we shouldn't. For some it's gossip; for others it's angry words. What area of controlling your tongue do you have most trouble with?

Does this tend to be directed at members of your family or at others?

Have you prayed and given this area to the Lord? What has He told you to do?

List three ways that you could gain better control over the things you say.

Are there any people you need to ask forgiveness of? If yes, make a plan to take care of that within the next few days or weeks.

Extending forgiveness or asking for forgiveness can also be a very sensitive maneuver. If we go to the person with hurt or angry feelings, what is most likely to come out is our hurt or anger. Being able to set an environment that allows forgiveness to flow freely is something only the Lord can achieve. And until we go to another person only in the power, forgiveness, and freedom of the Holy Spirit, we will not be able to give or receive forgiveness completely.

 KINGDOM EXTRA

The story of Joseph is an early account of the forgiving nature God expects us to display in our treatment of those who have wronged us. It is a founding example of Christlike love. Though Joseph's brothers sold him into slavery and deceived his father into thinking him dead, when he confronted his brothers during their time of need, his forgiveness and love burst forth from his heart. With uncanny faith in the overriding providence of God, he even professed his belief that God had used his brothers' betrayal of him as a means to deliver his family during the time of famine (v. 7). Joseph's forgiveness of his brothers' sin was so complete that he kissed all of them and wept with joy at being united with them once again. Brotherly forgiveness is expressive, self-giving, and offered in a way that assists its being received.[9]

FAITH ALIVE

You have made your plan to go and ask forgiveness of another person. Now is the time to ask the Lord exactly when you are to go, what you are to say, and to fill your heart with true repentance and the other person's heart with openness to receive what you have to say. Stop and ask the Lord to begin that work right now.

Finally, in maintaining relationships, we must realize that we never have the right to withhold forgiveness from another. Our heavenly Father never does that to us, and He calls His children continually to grow in becoming like Him.

KINGDOM EXTRA

These words are basic, yet their impact is intended to be life-changing at both points: 1) in our *receiving* God's love and merciful forgiveness and 2) in our *giving* it just as we have received it. Two virtues—goodness and forgiveness—are attributes birthed by our heavenly Father and expected to be found in our own lives. He expects us to be like Him—to stand ready to forgive our brother's transgressions in the same abundance of mercy He shows. "Abundant" is from the Hebrew *rab,* meaning "aboundingly, exceedingly." God does not want us to portion out our mercy and forgiveness with tea-spoons. He is looking for people who portion out their forgiveness and mercy with huge, unlimiting shovels.[10]

1. *Spirit-Filled Life Bible* (Nashville, TN: Thomas Nelson Publishers, 1991), 1567–1568, "Truth-In-Action through the Synoptic Gospels," #6.

2. Ibid., 1912, "Kingdom Dynamics: 1 Pet. 3:1–7, Attitudes Toward God Determine Attitudes Toward Mates."

3. Ibid., 1440–1441, "Kingdom Dynamics: Matt. 18:18–35, Forgiveness."

4. Ibid., 1260, "Kingdom Dynamics: Hosea 2:16, 17, 19, 20, Forgiveness Can Save and Transform a Marriage."

5. Ibid., 1712, "Kingdom Dynamics: Rom. 15:5–7, Receiving One Another Is the Way to Oneness."

6. Ibid., 790, "Truth-in-Action through Psalms (Book One: Psalms 1—41)," #7.

7. Ibid., 1798, "Truth-in-Action through Ephesians," #4.

8. Ibid., 1903, "Truth-in-Action through James," #4.

9. Ibid., 71, "Kingdom Dynamics: Gen. 45:4, Love Embraces Those Who Have Wronged Us."

10. Ibid., 827, "Kingdom Dynamics: Ps. 86:5, Abundantly Forgiven, Abundantly Forgive."

Lesson 12/Sex Is God's Idea

There is no greater confusion in our world today than the entire question of our sexuality as beings made in the image of God. The joy and power of the sexual relationship within marriage offer a boundless wealth to a couple in their life together. There is no surprise on God's part that sex is such a strong and compelling force in the human experience. The creative wonder of God's genius gave man not only the capacity to sustain the species but to use our sexuality to bring joy to and deepen the most intimate and desirable of all human relationships—that between husband and wife. The dynamic power of sex in its ability to fulfill the marriage relationship according to God's order has exactly the same power to destroy marriage and the family when it is disobediently indulged in outside of the marriage bond. With the Scriptures as our guide we will examine God's order regarding our sexuality. Understanding our sexuality must begin at its creation in the Garden of Eden.

Read Genesis 1:26–28. What was God's purpose in placing man on the planet?

With regard to gender, who bears the image of God?

Since both male and female bear the image of God, how does that influence God's understanding of our human needs as men and women?

What was God's first command to the first couple in Genesis 1:28?

Has God ever rescinded this command in the Bible?

What does this command reveal about the basic purpose and responsibility of human sexuality?

Now turn to Genesis 2:7–25. What were the two reasons given for the woman's creation in verse 18?

Why is it that God created partnership between a man and a woman?

Genesis 2:25 reveals an attitude about the human body. What was the response of the man and woman to their own nakedness and that of their partner?

Do you think God shares that same attitude about the human body?

Look at Genesis 3:7. When did the man and woman become self-conscious of their nakedness?

What brought about this response?

Was this embarrassment part of God's original design?

With the entrance of sin in the human experience came a breach of intimacy and self-consciousness about the sexual difference between male and female. How does sin in human experience continue to erode intimate relationships between marriage partners even today? Some have taught, erroneously, that the sin of the man and woman had to do with their discovery of sexual intimacy. What was the sin that brought such destruction into our world?

Do you think the issue was eating a piece of fruit or was it something greater? Explain your answer.

THE BLESSING OF SEX IN MARRIAGE

The Bible is remarkably candid about the joys of sexual intimacy between a husband and wife. "In the Song of Solomon, 'love' is the key word. This love, presenting the passionate desire between a man and a woman, King Solomon and the Shulamite, celebrates the joyous potential of marriage in light of sworn covenant principles. The basis for all human love should be covenant love, the master metaphor of the Bible. This covenant love is also the basis of the relationship between God and man; therefore, the Song applies properly to both marriage and to covenant history. The Shulamite therefore personifies the wife in an ideal marriage and the covenant people and their history in the Promised Land under the blessings of royal Solomonic love."[1]

The examination of this book of the Bible sets a liberating and fulfilling tone in the sexual relationship between a husband and wife. Read the Song of Solomon. As you read the book, what attitudes do you discover of this husband and wife toward each other?

Did you sense any embarrassment of the couple toward each other in their intimacy?

What was the response of the couple toward the physical attributes of their spouse?

Do you think these attitudes toward the physical aspects of a marriage relationship are appropriate and consistent with a holy life? Why or why not?

Do you think God is pleased with the openness of this couple with each other? Why or why not?

How does Solomon's bride view the coming of their wedding? (See 3:6–11.)

Obviously, there is considerable physical attraction between this couple. What do you think verse 10 means when it says, "Its interior is paved with love"?

Can sexual attraction be separated from love and still be healthy within marriage?

The Song of Solomon offers considerable instruction for married couples and for couples who are preparing for marriage. There are several principles related to a healthy family life which must be observed for there to be a maximum blessing in marriage.

Instruction one: Make an unshakable commitment to your marriage.

What is "the seal upon your heart" in 8:6?

In verse 8:7 a great sacrifice for love is described. What is it?

Instruction two: Healthy marital relations are secured in moral purity.

Read 1:2–4. Is sexual desire for your partner appropriate? Does it violate biblical moral purity? Explain your answer.

Read verses 2:7; 3:5; 8:4. All three verses use the phrase "Do not stir up nor awaken love until it pleases." What do you think this means?

Could these references refer to sexual relationships before marriage?

Instruction three: Spouses must accept each other without needing to change each other.

Read verses 1:15—2:1. What does this show about self-acceptance and acceptance of your partner?

What does 2:16 say about the matter of acceptance with each other?

Instruction four: Take time to address the problems and challenges every couple must face.

Are the "clefts of the rocks" and the "secret places of the cliff," as mentioned in 2:14, inevitable even in good marriages?

What do the "little foxes" in 2:15 represent in the life of this couple?

Instruction five: Learn to communicate your feelings openly and honestly with your partner.

Solomon is obviously delighted with his wife (4:8–15). How many different things does Solomon specifically refer to in describing his feeling about the Shulamite?

Does he say them directly to her?

Are all the things described by Solomon physical in this passage?

What is the Shulamite's response to her husband in 4:16?

Do you think this kind of open and intimate talk strengthens a marriage? Why or why not?

In the New Testament, guidelines are given to married couples about their sexual relationship. Read 1 Corinthians 7:2–5, and answer the questions below.

What does "due affection" mean in verse 3?

Why does the apostle say in verse 4 that a person does not have "authority over his own body"?

Who possesses this authority?

THE NEED TO TRAIN OUR CHILDREN

Another crucial aspect in the development of a healthy sexual relationship in marriage is directly related to how a person is trained to understand sexual relationships. The parental role in setting standards, communicating both the blessing and the responsibilities of our sexual life, and helping children develop healthy attitudes towards sex is the parent's responsibility. Too often the way children are trained about sexual matters is either through experience with their peers, self-discovery, or some sort of valueless sex-education curriculum provided in schools.

Every parent must be the primary source of information about sex for their children. It is unavoidable in our world to protect our children from other sources of sexual information. However, the role of the parent will determine the values of the child and provide them access to the most reliable and complete source of information about sex. Wherever the parent rejects this role as either embarrassing or inappropriate, someone else will eventually teach the child about sex. Then it is the values of another person which will begin to shape a crucial aspect of the relational development for the child, with life-long implications.

Read Deuteronomy 6:1–9.

What does "keep all His statutes and commandments" mean in verse 2?

Does this include God's view of moral purity?

Who are those who must keep these commandments in verse 2?

According to Deuteronomy 6:7, who is responsible to teach children the way of the Lord?

There are at least twenty benefits listed in Deuteronomy 7:12–26 resulting from obedience to the commandments of the Lord. List ten of them.

1.   6.

2.   7.

3.   8.

4.   9.

5.   10.

Is sexual purity one of the commandments which bring blessing?

Since the responsibility of teaching children about sex belongs with the parent, there is a question of what should be taught to the children and at what age. Here are five basic rules for communicating with our children about sex.

Rule One: Always answer the direct question your child asks about body anatomy and sexual relationship. These answers should be age appropriate. Young children should be answered with the minimum amount of information that satisfies their inquiry. If they are ready to know more specific information, they will ask. Volunteering more information than requested by the child can only confuse or disturb them with knowledge they are not able to process intellectually or emotionally.

Rule Two: Always answer truthfully. Answering questions about sexuality, childbirth, and the husband-wife relationship with embarrassed non-answers only communicates your own insecurity about sex to your children. It also demonstrates an absence of will to answer such sensitive questions, possibly leading your children to others who are more open to answering their questions.

Rule Three: Make a detailed presentation to your children about the facts of life before they receive this information from peers, school sex-education courses, etc. Parents have an enormous privilege to be the most trusted authority on sexual relationships with their children. Being forthright and honest opens the way for a healthy exchange of information, attitudes, values, and behavior as children become teenagers.

Rule Four: Communicate both the joy and God-given responsibility of the sexual relationship within marriage as your children reach their teen years. Any instructions on the mechanics of sexual function must be coupled directly with the responsibility of managing our lives according to the principles God has given us.

Rule Five: Make a covenant with your children about maintaining sexual purity before marriage. Knowing that Dad and Mom are willing and understanding prayer partners with them as they go through the challenging teenage years will provide a source of guidance and strength for young people navigating the waters of a sexually promiscuous and perverse world.

OBEDIENCE TO GOD'S SEXUAL LAWS

The Bible is specific about our sexual conduct. Repeatedly God warns us about the consequence of sexual activity outside of the sanctified relationship of marriage. However, the world's standard for sexual activity is markedly different. In this section we will study some specific aspects of God's law concerning sexual activity.

Adultery and Fornication

Read John 8:1–12. What is the sin of adultery?

WORD WEALTH

Adultery, *moicheia* (moy-*khi*-ah); *Strong's #3430:* Unlawful sexual intercourse, illicit connection with a married person, marital infidelity. *Moicheia* is incompatible with the harmonious laws of family life in God's kingdom; and since it violates God's original purpose in marriage, it is under God's judgment.[2]

What is the penalty for this sin according to verse 5? (See also Leviticus 20:10.)

Was the penalty in Leviticus 20:10 only for the woman?

Since this woman was caught "in adultery, in the very act" (8:4), why was her consort not taken to Jesus as well?

Were those who "caught" the woman interested in justice in this case?

What was Jesus' response to the adulterous woman in verse 11, 12?

Whom does Paul include in the list of the "unrighteous who will not inherit the kingdom of God" in 1 Corinthians 6:9?

What is a "fornicator" in 1 Corinthians 6:9?

WORD WEALTH

Fornications, *porneia* (por-*ni*-ah); *Strong's #4202:* Compare "pornography," "pornographic." Illicit sexual intercourse, including prostitution, whoredom, incest, licentiousness, adultery, and habitual immorality. The word describes both physical immorality and spiritual, signifying idolatry (Rev. 2:21; 14:8; 17:2).[3]

KINGDOM EXTRA

Sexual intercourse between a married person and someone who is not his or her mate is adultery. The Ten Commandments contain the prohibition against adultery: "You shall not commit adultery" (Ex. 20:14). The reason is simple: marriage is the foundation of society, and with it comes the responsibility of child-rearing. Casual sex outside marriage not only imperils marriage but also destroys the paternal or maternal feeling for the children of the marriage, and blurs the lines of family relationships.

Fornication is sex between two unmarried people. The apostle Paul taught that this is a sin against the body. He commanded Christians to flee fornication as a sin against self and God, for the believer's body is the temple of the Holy Spirit (1 Cor. 6:18, 19). Paul further wrote that if a believer takes his body and joins it to a harlot (or someone who is immoral), he is joining Jesus Christ to that person! (1 Cor. 6:15, 16).

It is extremely important to understand that neither fornicators nor adulterers will enter the kingdom of heaven (1 Cor. 6:9, 10). In today's world, the term *fornication* is rarely used, and immorality between unmarried people is commonly accepted as a life-style. But immorality, however commonplace, is a sin that will keep millions of people out of heaven, unless they repent.[4]

In 1 Corinthians 6:13–20 why is the apostle Paul so adamant about sexual purity for the people of God?

What is the instruction in verse 18 for people who are tempted with immorality?

In verse 20 we are instructed to glorify God. How?

Read Matthew 5:27–30. Jesus redefines adultery in verse 28. How?

Jesus teaches us that adultery begins in the heart due to our lust. He also uses the metaphor of plucking out an eye or cutting off a hand to stop such lust. What point is the Lord making with such imagery?

KINGDOM EXTRA

Jesus does not stop short at overt adultery, but points to adulterous desire. He demands complete self-control over the members of the body. He does not prescribe literal self-mutilation, but a rigid, moral self-denial.[5]

Homosexuality

Read Romans 1:18–32. In verses 26, 27, the sin of homosexuality is described by four different sets of terms, what are they?

1.   3.

2.   4.

The commitment to violate God's way in sexual obedience is described in its beginning in verse 21. What are the two things people do in this verse to reject God?

What does the Bible say in verse 32 about those who practice the acts listed in this passage? (Also see Lev. 20:13.)

Romans 1:32 describes judgment not only for those who practice such wickedness but for those who "approve of those who practice them." Why is this so?

Incest and Sexual Abuse

Read Leviticus 18 and 20. As you read these specific laws about sexual purity within family relationships, it is clear that the only God-sanctioned sexual relationship is between husband and wife. Much damage has been done throughout the ages by lust-filled, demonically-inspired incest. It destroys the trust in the family. The devastation of lives has brought much pain to so many as a result of those who have violated God's order in the family. Why is God so specific about purity of sexual relationships within the family?

What does the Bible say about lust for a family member that does not produce the result of physical adultery?

Job 31:1

Prov. 6:25

Matt. 5:28

James 1:14–16

Self-Control and Masturbation

There is some controversy in the church over the propriety of masturbation for the single person. Clearly, masturbation denies the proper consideration of one spouse for the other in marriage and is thereby not appropriate. However, for the single person there are several considerations which must be addressed on this matter.

What two things does 1 John 2:16 say about "the lust of the flesh, the lust of the eyes, and the pride of life?"

First John 2:17 declares that the lust of the world is:

According to verse 17, who will abide forever?

Read Ephesians 4:17–24. In verse 17 we are told not to walk in the way that the rest of the Gentiles walk. There are seven things that characterize this walk. What are they?

1.   5.

2.   6.

3.   7.

4.

Verse 19 describes a self-willed attitude toward sex and perversion. Paul uses one phrase and three words to characterize this behavior; list them.

1.   3.

2.   4.

Is masturbation possible without lust, or does it open the door to it?

Read Galatians 5:16–26. How does self-control in verse 23 relate to the sex life of the believer who is unmarried?

How is this kind of self-control possible according to verses 16, 24, and 25?

1. Walk _____.

2. Crucify _____.

3. Live _____.

Read 1 Corinthians 7:1, 2, 8, 9. Do you think the apostle Paul understands the difficulties single people encounter with sexual purity?

Read 1 Corinthians 7:8, 25–40. Do you think it is possible that some people use their own self-gratification to avoid the responsibility of marriage and a family? How do you think they do this?

We've talked about some very sensitive issues in this chapter, yet they must be addressed from a biblical perspective. In reviewing the scriptures you've looked up, what areas of your life is the Lord challenging you to change? Are they areas of addition or deletion? How will these changes affect your relationship with your spouse, if you have one?

As you present these areas to the Lord, ask Him to show you how to incorporate these changes into your life and give you the strength and steadfastness to live your life according to His commands.

1. *The Spirit-Filled Life Bible* (Nashville, TN: Thomas Nelson Publishers, 1991), 946, "Introduction to the Song of Solomon, Purpose."

2. Ibid., 1588, "Word Wealth John 8:3 adultery."

3. Ibid., 1434, "Word Wealth John 15:19 fornications."

4. Ibid., 2003, "Spiritual Answers to Hard Questions #18."

5. Ibid., 1412, note on Matt. 5:28–30.

Lesson 13/Spiritual Life of a Family

Hosts of people face marriage, parenthood, and the governing of their homes completely mystified as to how God's kingdom can come abide where they are. It's said that we face these situations like our parents did because they are our role models. That can be a frightening prospect for many whose parents were physically or emotionally abusive, substance dependent, relationally dysfunctional, or simply unbelieving. But the Scriptures reveal that we are no longer bound to our past!

NEW LIFE, NEW FAMILY

Since we have been born again into a new family, who is now our Father? (Gal. 4:6)

Turn to Romans 4:16. Who is also called our Father?

Abraham, like many of us, faced a situation in which he had to learn to live a new life-style apart from an unbelieving family. Read Genesis 12:1–3 and write down what was God's command to him, along with what God promised to do through him.

Not only did Abraham go to live in a new country and adopt a new lifestyle, what else drastically changed in Abraham's life:

Gen. 17:5

Gen. 17:10–11

 KINGDOM EXTRA

Abraham is shown in both Old Testament and New Testament as the prototype of all who experience God's processes of seeking to reinstate man through redemption, first and foremost, in his relationship to God by faith, without words (Rom. 4:1–25). But too seldom is the second facet of redemption noted. Abraham is also shown as a case of God's program to recover man's "reign in life" (Rom. 5:17). Abraham is designated as the "father" of all who walk his pathway of faith (Rom. 4:12). As such, he is God's revealed example of His plan to eventually reestablish His kingdom's rule in all the Earth through people of His covenant. Through Abraham, whom He wills to become "a great nation" (restoring rule) and to whom He chooses to give a "great name" (restoring authority), God declares His plans to beget innumerable children who will be modeled after this prototypical "father of faith." This truth is confirmed in Romans 4:13, where Abraham's designation as "heir of the world" parallels Jesus' promise that His followers, who humble themselves in faith, shall also be recipients of "the kingdom" and shall "inherit the earth" (Matt 5:3-5).[1]

Through Abraham's life, we can also see very practical ways that he led his family spiritually. Look up the following verses and write down the aspects of spiritual life that we see lived out by Abraham. (The first one is done for you.)

Rom. 4:3   believing God (and His Word)

Gen. 14:14–17

Gen. 14:18

Gen. 15:13–21; 18:16–21 (Compare these verses with 1 Cor. 12:7–11.)

Gen. 18:22–33

Gen. 20:17

Go back over the above list. Which of these aspects of spiritual life do you feel are currently active in your family life? As we continue through this study, note the areas where your family needs to grow spiritually and begin formulating a plan of action.

WORSHIP IN THE FAMILY

We see worship many times throughout Abraham's life as he obeyed the Lord, believed His Word, and built altars to make covenants and offer sacrifices. In many respects his life was lived out in the spirit of worship. But that is seen no more clearly than when, at the command of the Lord, he went to worship prepared to offer Isaac as the sacrifice. It is obvious in reading this account that Isaac was familiar with the procedures of the worship process.

 KINGDOM EXTRA

Psalm 145:4 emphasizes the importance of passing on the praise of God from one generation to another. Praise is to be taught to our children. The Bible enjoins us to raise a generation of praisers. We must not merely "suppose" that children will grow up and desire God. We must be careful. Whatever we possess of God's blessing and revelation can be lost in one generation. We must consistently praise Him and we must also teach (by example, as well as by words), so our children and our children's children will do the same.[2]

Read Gen. 22:1–14 and note the lessons that Isaac would have learned from his father. What was Abraham's immediate response to the Lord when he received this startling command? (vv. 1–3)

How do we see Isaac's parallel obedience in verse 9?

What does verse 5 tell us about the practice of worship in Abraham's home?

How does verse 7 show that Isaac was familiar with Abraham's worship practices?

 KINGDOM EXTRA

Isaac was born to Abraham and Sarah as a result of covenant promise (Gen. 17:1). God's requirement of Abraham to sacrifice Isaac was the supreme test that would demonstrate both Abraham's reverence for God and his confidence in God's faithfulness to keep His covenant promise. He prepared to offer up Isaac with the assurance the God would raise him from death itself (Heb. 11:19). God made a timely intervention and provided a ram to be sacrificed instead of Isaac. This is a dramatic foreshadowing of God's offering His only begotten Son to die in our place (John 3:16). God's covenant love gave Abraham a son, and covenant love provided a substitutionary sacrifice to save that son. Centuries later covenant love would cause God to give His own Son as a blood sacrifice for the sons of men.[3]

Later in Genesis, we read that God's covenant with Abraham was restated to Isaac (26:2–5). What understanding of God's covenant promise do you think Isaac showed in chapter 22?

What kind of sacrifice does Hebrews 13:15 tell us that we are to offer now?

KINGDOM EXTRA

Why is praising God a sacrifice? The word "sacrifice" (Greek *thusia*) comes from the root *thuo,* a verb meaning "to kill or slaughter for a purpose." Praise often requires that we "kill" our pride, fear, or sloth—anything that threatens to diminish or interfere with our worship of the Lord. We also discover here the basis of all our praise: the sacrifice of our Lord Jesus Christ. It is by Him, in Him, with Him, to Him, and for Him that we offer our sacrifice of praise to God. Praise will never be successfully hindered when we keep its focus on Him—the Founder and Completer of our salvation. His Cross, His Blood—His love gift and forgiveness to us—keep praise as a *living* sacrifice.[4]

FAITH ALIVE

Does your family praise the Lord together? How do you do that?

What are some ways you can incorporate praise naturally into your family life?

Why do you think that praising the Lord in your home is important spiritually? emotionally? mentally?

THE FAMILY THAT PRAYS TOGETHER

In Genesis 18:22–33 we see Abraham interceding for Sodom—and thus for his nephew, Lot and his family. Likewise we are called to prayer. Our pattern for prayer is given in Luke 11:2–4. Read the Lord's Prayer in Luke 11:2–4. List the different topics covered in the prayer:

    KINGDOM EXTRA

Jesus' words "Your kingdom come" are more than a suggestion to pray for a distant millennial day, for everything in this prayer is current. This prayer is not a formula for repetition so much as it is an outline for expansion. Worship is to be longer than a sentence. Petitions are not confined to bread. Forgiveness is to be requested in specifics, not generalities, and prayer for the entry of God's kingdom into present earthborn situations is not accomplished in a momentary utterance. The verb mood and tense of "Your Kingdom come" essentially says, "Father, let Your kingdom come here and now!"

Such prayerful *intervention* is called *intercession*. Motivation toward such prayer occurs when we recognize the importance Jesus placed on prayer in helping us serve in our roles as "kingdom administrators." Without the intervention of God's kingdom rule through prayer, Earth's circumstances will succumb to inevitable consequences. Earthly scenes of need must be penetrated by God's "will here as in heaven." Either the weakness of man's rule (the flesh) or the viciousness of hell's works (the devil) will prevail. God's power alone can change things and bring heaven's rule (kingdom) instead, and the honor and the glory for prayer's answers are His. However, the praying is ours to do: unless we ask for the intervention of His kingdom and obey His prayer-lessons, nothing will change. All kingdom ministry begins with, is sustained by, and will triumph through prayer.[5]

Look up the following verses and write down what they promise prayer will accomplish:

Matt. 17:21

Acts 10:4

Phil. 4:6

James 5:15, 16

> When are we supposed to pray?

Luke 18:1

1 Thess. 5:17

> For what are we supposed to pray?

Ps. 122:6

Matt. 5:44; 9:38; 26:41

Luke 22:40

Heb. 13:18

> Who helps us to pray?

Romans 8:26

Our family prays together a lot: mealtimes, bedtime, on the way to school, when we get an urgent phone call, when someone is sick, baseball games, church, throughout the day for one another. When does your family pray?

Are these times of freedom and openness, or are they embarrassing and awkward for one or more family members?

What are some ways you can make prayer times more natural in your home? Or is there resistance to participation?

As we move our families into a more active prayer life we must recognize that as spiritual leaders within our own families, a change in prayer habits will have to begin with us.

SHARING THE LORD'S TABLE

First Corinthians 11:24-25 tells us that we are to share the Lord's Table "in remembrance of Me" (Jesus). There are multiplied times in the course of a family's life that we need to remember what Jesus has accomplished for us through His death and what He calls us to live in through His life. We need to remember that healing is provided for us through the Cross when someone is sick. We need to remember that He is our Provider for all things when finances are low. We need to remember that He is our Forgiver when we've sinned against one another. And the list could go on forever.

In Genesis 14:18, we see Abraham partaking of the bread and cup as Melchizedek, the priest of the Most High God, comes out to bless him following a battle.

Read 1 Corinthians 11:23–30 and answer the following questions. What are we supposed to be remembering when we partake?

Do you think we are just supposed to be reviewing the events that took place at the Cross, or are we to be praising God for what was accomplished there, or both? Explain your answer.

Verses 27–29 give a severe and somber warning to us. What do you think this warning means?

What kind of attitude toward Communion do you think is required as we come to the table?

Read verse 30. What does this have to do with receiving Communion?

Is it possible that some people are sick because they simply haven't received the healing that is available to them through the Cross?

KINGDOM EXTRA

Just as the act of water baptism outwardly declares or confesses an inward experience of salvation through the blood of the Lord Jesus, each observance of the Lord's Table is a powerful occasion for faith's confession. In the ordinance, the Christian confesses before all heaven that he not only has believed, but that he has not forgotten. "In remembrance" involves more than just memory; the word suggests an "active calling to mind" (Wycliffe).

The word "for" introduces the reason the Supper is continually repeated. It is an acted sermon, for it "proclaims" the Lord's death. The outward act of faith, as the bread and cup taken, is explicitly said to be an ongoing, active confession—literally "you are *proclaiming*" (v. 26). Each occasion of partaking is an opportunity to say, proclaim, or *confess* again: "I herewith lay hold of all the benefits of Jesus Christ's full redemption for my life—forgiveness, wholeness, strength, health, sufficiency." The Lord's Supper is not to be simply a ritual remembrance, but an active confession, by which you actively will to call to memory and appropriate *today* all that Jesus has provided and promised through His Cross.[6]

THE WORD IN OUR FAMILIES

Abraham didn't have the benefit we have of having God's written Word to study. But he lived by God's spoken Word to him and patterned his life after God's Word in every area. Copy Romans 4:20, 21 to see how Abraham lived his life.

WORD WEALTH

Abraham had learned to "live his life by the *logos* of God." Most of us are familiar with the Greek word, *logos,* which describes the Word of God in its various demonstrations. *Strong's* (*#3056*) defines *logos* as a transmission of thought, communication, a word of explanation, an utterance, discourse, divine revelation, talk, statement, instruction, an oracle, divine promise, divine doctrine, divine declaration. Jesus is the living *logos* (John 1:1); the Bible is the written *logos* (Heb. 4:12); and the Holy Spirit utters the spoken *logos* (1 Cor. 2:13).[7]

   FAITH ALIVE

Look up the following verses that tell of times the Lord spoke to Abraham. What did God say and what did Abraham do?

Gen. 12:1–8

Gen. 13:14–18

Gen. 15:1—6

Gen. 17:1–10, 23–27

Gen. 18:10–15, 21:1–4

Gen. 22:1–14

Does the Lord speak to you this clearly today? If not, do you think He wants to?

How do you think hearing God's voice (either through vision, impression, or Scripture) would affect your family life? How did it affect Abraham's?

List several ways the Lord has spoken to you in regard to your family. What were the results?

KINGDOM EXTRA

We are all inexperienced in too much of life to be without a guide. God's Word is that guide. The entirety of Psalm 119 unfolds manifold features of God's Word, showing how dynamically it will assist us in life's most practical circumstances. But no single verse focuses this more clearly than verse 105, which shows how God's Word lights the way, giving direction for each *step* ("to my feet") and giving wisdom for *long-range plans* ("to my path"). Joshua links the regular application of God's Word to life as the most certain way to both success and prosperity in living (Josh. 1:8). Further, Psalm 119:130 notes the wisdom God's Word gives to the "simple" (Hebrew *pethawee*), a truth specifically pointing toward the avoidance of making decisions based on human delusion or outright senselessness. Also, Proverbs 6:23 reminds us that the "reproofs" or corrections the Bible gives are as much a part of the "light" it provides as any positive or confirming direction we find therein. Let God's Word guide, correct, instruct, lead, teach, and confirm. Do not hasten ahead without it—*ever.*[8]

A miscalculation parents often make is to assume that their children will simply "absorb the Word" in the environment of a believing home. Or they believe that what their children receive at Sunday School each week will be enough to teach them the basic beliefs and doctrines of Scriptures. But, as with most other areas of our children's lives, it requires much more of us. The Word in our families must be lived out in front of them. It requires teaching, explaining, demonstrating, applying, illustrating, proving, memorizing—literally embodying all that scripture can mean in our lives. As we do this, we will be begin to see incorporated into our homes and our children's lives the great peace that the Bible promises for those who love God's law (see Ps. 119:165).

   ### FAITH ALIVE

What are you currently doing to help your children learn and incorporate the Word into their lives?

What are some things you could begin doing to accomplish this task?

List three ways that you have seen the peace of the Holy Spirit permeate your home as a result of the Word.

SPIRITUAL WARFARE FOR THE FAMILY

In Genesis 14:14-17, we see Abraham going to battle for the rescue of Lot and his family. In Abraham's case, he went to an actual battle against actual territorial rulers. Who or what are we to do battle against?

Eph. 6:12

1 Pet. 5:8

Praise God, He doesn't leave us defenseless against our adversary. In Ephesians 6:10–18, the apostle Paul lists the armor and weapons that we are to put on. What are they?

  WORD WEALTH

Paul admonishes us to put on the whole armor of God in order to stand against the forces of hell. It is clear that our warfare is not against physical forces, but against invisible powers who have clearly defined levels of authority in a real, though invisible, sphere of activity. Paul, however, not only warns us of a clearly defined structure in the invisible realm, he instructs us to take up the whole armor of God in order to maintain a "battle-stance" against this unseen satanic structure. All of this armor is not just a passive protection in facing the enemy; it is to be used offensively against these satanic forces. Note Paul's final directive: we are to be "praying always with all prayer and supplication in the Spirit" (v. 18). Thus, prayer is not so much a weapon, or even a part of the armor, as it is the means by which we engage in the battle itself and the purpose for which we are armed. To put on the armor of God is to prepare for battle. Prayer is the battle itself, with God's Word being our chief weapon employed against Satan during our struggle.[9]

FAITH ALIVE

In our culture, the battle for the family can engage at almost any dimension from substance abuse and violence to attitudes and disobedience to negative media influences and overwork. In your family life, right now, where do you feel the greatest battle is being waged?

Has the Lord given you specific directives in prayer to see this battle through to its conclusion?

Write down a promise from God's Word that promises victory in that area.

KINGDOM EXTRA

In Matthew 11:12, Jesus asserts the "violence" of the kingdom. The unique grammatical construction of the text does not make clear if the kingdom of God is the victim of violence or if, as the kingdom advances in victory, it does so through violent spiritual conflict and warfare. But the context does. Jesus' references to the nonreligious style of John and the confrontive, miraculous ministry of Elijah teach that the kingdom of God makes its penetration by a kind of violent entry opposing the human status quo. It transcends the "softness" (v. 8) of staid religious formalism and exceeds the pretension of child's play (vv. 16, 17). It refuses to "dance to the music" of society's expectation that the religious community provide either entertainment ("we played the flute") or dead traditionalism ("we mourned").

Jesus defines the "violence" of His kingdom's expansion by defining the "sword" and "fire" He has brought as different from the battle techniques of political or military warfare (compare Matt. 10:34–39 and Luke 12:49–53 with John 18:36). The upheaval caused by the kingdom of God is not caused by political provocation or armed advance. It is the result of God's order shaking relationships, households, cities, and nations by the entry of the Holy Spirit's power working in people. (See also Luke 16:16).[10]

We are never to hesitate to minister or move into warfare. We have been empowered by Jesus Himself! But remember that ministry begins at home.

SPIRITUAL GIFTS IN THE FAMILY

Too often, our concept of the operation of spiritual gifts is confined to miraculous healing or the giving of a tongue and interpretation. And while spiritual gifts obviously cover those areas, it can extend to much more—especially in our families!

In Genesis 18:16–33, we see Abraham receive a spiritual gift in the form of a word of knowledge: the Lord simply told Abraham what He was about to do so Abraham could intercede. In raising our children, we have often received such gifts in regard to our kids' attitudes, life choices, turning points, friends, and spiritual lives. We've even had the Lord show us things about such practical areas as their health, grades, and sleep needs. God is intensely interested about every area of our lives and is ready and willing to give us guidance in those areas if we will turn to Him.

 **FAITH ALIVE**

Turn to 1 Corinthians 12:7–10 and list the nine gifts of the Holy Spirit.

Are there ways that you have seen any of these gifts operate within the life of your family? What are they?

Do you feel fearful or hesitant in any way about the gifts of the Holy Spirit functioning within your family? Why?

How does the instruction and encouragement in 1 Corinthians 12 answer to any fears you may have?

What are some ways you could invite the function of these gifts into your family? (i.e., When someone is sick, you could make prayer for healing your "first resort" rather than the doctor).

A Word About Healing

Christians, in their zeal, can sometimes overlook the practical wisdom of going to the doctor. They disregard the fact that the Lord may be giving them a gift of wisdom in going to the doctor, where He wants to work a gift of healing to them through the doctor! All good gifts come from the Father (James 1:17), and it's fairly safe to say that something (medicine) and someone (doctor) who helps make people well is a good gift. So pray first, but if the Lord tells you to go to the doctor, don't feel like your faith has failed. Go believing that this is how God wants to work healing to your family this time!

 ### Faith Alive

We've only scratched the surface of the lessons we could learn from the life of our father, Abraham. For example, Abraham also treated his extended family unselfishly

(13:7–11), refused to compromise (14:22–24; 24:6); kept his children in right priority before the Lord (22:1–14); had his finances in order (14:20), and had an ordered relationship with his wife (1 Pet. 3:6). Even through Abraham's failing we learn lessons of a man ready to right wrongs (20:7–18), and of the Lord's faithfulness to single mothers (21:16–20). Plan to take some time over the next days to examine Abraham's life more closely and write down other lessons we could learn from him. Genesis 11:26—25:10 covers the life of Abraham, but he is mentioned throughout the Bible. Here are some other scripture references to help you start:

Rom. 4:1–16

Gal. 3:6–18

Heb. 11:8–19

James 2:21–23

1. *Spirit-Filled Life Bible* (Nashville, TN: Thomas Nelson Publishers, 1991), 22, "Kingdom Dynamics: Gen. 12:1–3, 'Prototype' Kingdom Person."

2. Ibid., 876, "Kingdom Dynamics: Ps. 145:4, Teach Your Children Praise."

3. Ibid., 36, "Kingdom Dynamics: Gen. 22:13, Isaac, the Result of Covenant."

4. Ibid., 1890, "Kingdom Dynamics: Heb. 13:10–15, The Sacrifice of Praise."

5. Ibid., 1535, "Kingdom Dynamics: Luke 11:2–4, Prayer and Intercession."

6. Ibid., 1735, "Kingdom Dynamics: 1 Cor. 11:23–26, Faith at the Lord's Table."

7. Ibid., 1665, "Word Wealth Acts 19:20 word."

8. Ibid., 860, "Kingdom Dynamics: Ps. 119:105, God's Word and Practical, Fruitful Living."

9. Ibid., 1797, "Kingdom Dynamics: Eph. 6:10–18, Spiritual Warfare."

10. Ibid., 1424, "Kingdom Dynamics: Matt. 11:12, Taking It by Force."